stōry Items

1. the men did not lift the .
   - car   • cat   (• cow)

2. the cow said, "I can lift ."
   - a car   (• mē)   • men

Wh	Wh	Wh	Wh	Wh	Wh	Wh
m	m	m	m	m	m	m
th	th	th	th	th	th	th
r	r	r	r	r	r	r
Sh	Sh	Sh	Sh	Sh	Sh	Sh
a	a	a	a	a	a	a

1. the man can **run** .

2. the girl can **run** .

3. the dog līkes to **sit** .

1

---

stōry Items

1. a fat dog met a little .
   - (• dog)   • pig   • gōat

2. the little dog did not līke her red .
   - dog   • fēēt   (• nōse)

Sh	Sh	Sh	Sh	Sh	Sh	Sh
Wh	Wh	Wh	Wh	Wh	Wh	Wh
n	n	n	n	n	n	n
th	th	th	th	th	th	th
r	r	r	r	r	r	r
o	o	o	o	o	o	o

1. the man is **fat** .

2. the cat is on his **hat** .

3. sō the man is **mad** .

1. the girl lIkes to **run** _____ .

2. shē has a **cat** _____ .

3. the cat has a **hat** _____ .

1. a **girl** _____ is nēar the lāke.

2. shē has a **dog** _____ .

2

1. mom has a **dog** _____ .

2. the dog sēēs a **cat** _____ .

3. the dog is **mad** _____ .

1. the girl has a **fan** _____ .

2. her cat has a **hat** _____ .

i	i	i	i	i	i	i
m	m	m	m	m	m	m
w	w	w	w	w	w	w
s	s	s	s	s	s	s
t	t	t	t	t	t	t
v	v	v	v	v	v	v

hē had a pāint can.

hē had a pāint can.

he had a paint can.

he had a paint can.

he had a paint can.

Also accept pāint with long line.

r	r	r	r	r	r	r
t	t	t	t	t	t	t
y	y	y	y	y	y	y
u	u	u	u	u	u	u
e	e	e	e	e	e	e
a	a	a	a	a	a	a

I wish I had a dog.

I wish I had a dog.

I wish I had a dog.

I wish I had a dog.

I wish I had a dog.

stŏry Items

1. a girl met a fat ▨▨▨▨▨ .

  • can   ⬤ cat   • girl

2. did the cat lIke fish căke?

  ⬤ yes   • nŏ

1. that **cat** lIkes to ĕat.

2. shē is on a **bed** .

wh — Wh Wh Wh Wh Wh Wh

s — s s s s s s

th — th th th th th th

ē — ē ē ē ē ē ē

sh — sh sh sh sh sh sh

u — u u u u u u

that cat can talk.
that cat can talk.
that cat can talk.
that cat can talk.
that cat can talk.

3

---

stŏry Items

1. the dog lived in the ▨▨▨▨▨ .

  ⬤ yard   • farm   • hut

2. the cop said, "I nĕĕd a ▨▨▨▨▨ dog."

  • cap   • fat   ⬤ cop

1. the man got a **fish** .

2. the **boy** is in the ship.

i — i i i i i i

th — th th th th th th

e — e e e e e e

wh — Wh Wh Wh Wh Wh Wh

u — u u u u u u

n — n n n n n n

dig a big hōle.
dig a big hōle.
dig a big hole.
dig a big hole.
dig a big hole.

Also accept hōle with long line.

stŏry Items

1. a man had an ▨▨▨▨ car.
   - tōld   (• ōld)   • gōld

2. the big man mãde the car ▨▨▨▨ .
   - sit   (• start)   • red

1. this **boy** is in the mud.

2. his mom is **mad** .

w w w w w w w
o o o o o o o
i i i i i i i
m m m m m m m
a a a a a a a
wh wh wh wh wh wh wh

I lIke ōld cars.
I līke ōld cars.
I like old cars.
I like old cars.
I like old cars.

---

rēadĭng

the dog went in the yard.

the dog dug a big hōle.

1. the dog went in the ▨▨▨▨ .
   - lãke   (• yard)   • yēar

2. hē dug a big ▨▨▨▨ .
   - log   • yard   (• hōle)

1. the girl has a toy **car** .

2. the **boy** is in the mud.

3. hē is **mad** .

a a a a a a a a
b b b b b b b
c c c c c c c
d d d d d d d
e e e e e e e
f f f f f f f

sēē if it will start.
sēē if it will start.
see if it will start.
see if it will start.
see if it will start.

reading

shē went to get fish.

but shē cāme back with a can.

1. shē went to get ▦▦▦▦.
   - • sick   • fins   (• fish)

2. but shē cāme back with a ▦▦▦▦.
   - • fan   (• can)   • cāke

1. the boy has a **can** _____.

2. the girl has a **fan** _____.

3. the dog lIkes to **sit** _____.

---

e e e e e e e
f f f f f f f
g g g g g g g
h h h h h h h
i i i i i i i
J J J J J J J

hē went down the rōad.

he went down the road.

he went down the road.

he went down the road.

he went down the road.

5

---

stŏry Items

1. the dog's nāme was ▦▦▦▦.
   - (• sal)   • sāme   • cāme

2. the dog lIked to ▦▦▦▦ books.
   - (• rēad)   • red   • ēat

1. this **cat** _____ is not sad.

2. shē has a **hat** _____.

th	th th th	t	t t t
s	s s s	i	i i i
f	f f f	u	u u u

---

reading

shē fell with a pāint can.

now shē has a whIte nōse.

1. shē ▦▦▦▦ with a pāint can.
   - • fill   • ran   (• fell)

2. now shē has a whIte ▦▦▦▦.
   - (• nōse)   • ēar   • foot

whȳ not tāke a bath?

whȳ not tāke a bath?

why not take a bath?

why not take a bath?

why not take a bath?

why not take a bath?

stŏry Items

1. arf was a barking ▦▦▦▦▦ .
   - card   ⊙ (shark)   - farm

2. a big ▦▦▦ swam up to the other sharks.
   (⊙ fish)   - fin   - fan

---

shē is in a car.

shē is in a car.

shē is in a car.

shē is in a car.

n	n n n	h	h h h
u	u u u	w	w w w
m	m m m	v	v v v

rēading

a boy āte cāke.

hē got sick.

1. a ▦▦▦▦ āte cāke.
   - man   ⊙ (boy)   - girl

2. hē got ▦▦▦▦ .
   (⊙ sick)   - sad   - wet

---

1. this **man** ____ is ŏld.

2. hē has a **rug** ____ .

1. the **boy** ____ is in the trēē.

2. the **pig** ____ is in the trēē.

---

stŏry Items

1. arf had to ▦▦▦▦ the other sharks.
   - hēar   ⊙ (help)   - hŏld

2. arf swam up to the big ▦▦▦▦ .
   - farm   - fat   ⊙ (fish)

3. do the other sharks līke arf now?
   (⊙ yes)   - nŏ

---

arf was a shark.

arf was a shark.

arf was a shark.

arf was a shark.

h	h h h	i	i i i
n	n n n	a	a a a
m	m m m	o	o o o

rēading

wē ran in the rāin.

wē had wet fēēt.

1. wē ran in the ▦▦▦▦ .
   - rŏad   ⊙ (rāin)   - lāke

2. ▦▦▦▦ had wet fēēt.
   - you   - mē   ⊙ (wē)

---

1. the **dog** ____ is gŏing for the pig.

2. that pig has a **hat** ____ .

1. a **man** ____ is in the car.

2. a **pig** ____ is on the car.

reading

fIve fish went fŏr a swim.

they met a shark nāmed arf.

1. fIve fish went ░░░░░.
   - to a lāke
   - fŏr a fish
   - **(fŏr a swim)**

2. they met a ░░░░░.
   - ship
   - bark
   - **(shark)**

a farmer had an ōld cow.

the farmer sat, and the cow went to slēēp.

1. a farmer had an ░░░░░.
   - ōld hat
   - **(ōld cow)**
   - ōld how

2. the cow ░░░░░.
   - sat
   - went to the farm
   - **(went to slēēp)**

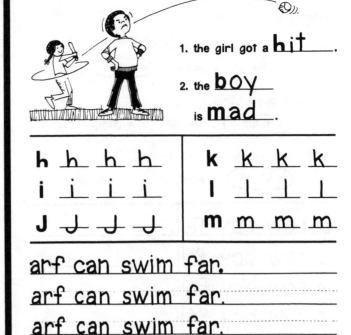

1. the girl got a **hit** _____.

2. the **boy** _____ is **mad** _____.

h h h h	k k k k
i i i i	l l l l
J J J J	m m m m

arf can swim far.
arf can swim far.
arf can swim far.
arf can swim far.
arf can swim far.
arf can swim far.

7

---

stŏry Items

1. a cow boy did not have a ░░░░░.
   - cow
   - hat
   - **(hŏrse)**

2. then the cow boy got on a ░░░░░.
   - **(cow)**
   - cat
   - car

3. the other cow boys said, "░░░░░."
   - gō, gō
   - **(hō, hō)**
   - nō, nō

hē had a cow.
he had a cow.
he had a cow.
he had a cow.

s s s s	f f f f
t t t t	l l l l
r r r r	i i i i

the girls ran with a dog. the dog

ran and ran. the girls had to stop.

1. the girls ran with a ░░░░░.
   - **(dog)**
   - gŏat
   - man

2. the ░░░░░ had to stop.
   - men
   - **(girls)**
   - dog

a farmer had a cow. the cow had

a pet. the pet was a bug.

1. a farmer had a ░░░░░.
   - bell
   - **(cow)**
   - bug

2. the cow had a pet ░░░░░.
   - but
   - dog
   - **(bug)**

1. the man has big **feet** _____.

2. the girl has a **hat** _____.

stōry Items

1. the cow boys rōde to a ░░░░░░░ .
   - lāke   - pond   - (crēēk)

2. a cow boy's hōrse ░░░░░░░ .
   - (stopped)   - slid   - jumped

3. the cow boy on the cow said, "░░░░░░░ ."
   - (hō, hō)   - nō, nō   - sō, sō

---

a cow boy fell.
a cow boy fell.
a cow boy fell.
a cow boy fell.

Wh wh wh wh	a a a a
th th th th	u u u u
sh sh sh sh	i i i i

8

a bug got mad at a cat. the bug said,
"I will bIte you." so the bug bit the cat.

1. a ░░░░░░░ got mad at a cat.
   - ran   - cat   - (bug)

2. sō the bug ░░░░░░░ the cat.
   - bIte   - hit   - (bit)

I went to slēēp in a barn. a cow
kissed my hand. I lIke that cow.

1. I went to ░░░░░░░ in a barn.
   - run   - sit   - (slēēp)

2. A cow kissed my ░░░░░░░ .
   - (hand)   - fēēt   - nōse

---

1. shē has a little **fish** _____ .

2. hē has a **big** _____ fish.

---

stōry Items

1. did a hōrse jump the crēēk?
   - yes   - (no)

2. the cow ran up to the ░░░░░░░ of the crēēk.
   - sIde   - (bank)   - top

---

then the cow jumped.
then the cow jumped.
then the cow jumped.
then the cow jumped.

ā ā ā ā	r r r r
ō ō ō ō	s s s s
d d d d	b b b b

shē lIked to walk. sō shē walked in
the park. shē met a girl and a dog.

1. shē lIked to ░░░░░░░ .
   - sit   - park   - (walk)

2. shē met a girl and a ░░░░░░░ .
   - man   - (dog)   - cat

---

wē got a little rabbit.
that rabbit jumped.

1. ░░░░░░░ got a little rabbit.
   - you   - (wē)   - mē

2. that ░░░░░░░ jumped.
   - cow   - dog   - (rabbit)

1. the little **bug** _____ is in the can.

2. the big bug is **not** _____ in the can.

story Items

1. the jumped ōver the crēēk.
   - hŏrse   • bank   (• cow)

2. the cow boy gāve the cow a .
   - car   (• kiss)   • hŏrse

hē kissed his cow.
hē kissed his cow.
hē kissed his cow.
hē kissed his cow.

d	d d d	s	s s s
J	J J J	t	t t t
b	b b b	m	m m m

---

shē was not fat. shē had a hat.
shē sat on a cat.

1. was not fat.
   - mē   • sēē   (• shē)

2. shē sat on a .
   - (• cat)   • rat   • hat

---

the cow āte fīve hot cākes.
shē did not get sick.

1. the āte hot cākes.
   - (• cow)   • cat   • cāke

2. shē did not get .
   - fat   (• sick)   • sad

1. the man is **not** little.

2. his **dog** is little.

9

---

1. māke r in the circle.

2. māke s in the box.

(r)   [S]

---

a girl went fishing. but shē did not
get fish at the crēēk. shē got wet.

1. shē went .
   - running   • walking   (• fishing)

2. but shē did not get fish at .
   - the lāke   • hōme   (• the crēēk)

---

a cow had a cōld. sō the cow got
a book. then the cow went to bed.

1. the cow had a .
   - gōld   (• cōld)   • hōld

2. then the cow went to .
   - a book   (• bed)   • the boy

1. the **cow** can jump.

2. the men are **wet**.

3. the **cow boy**
   on the cow is happy.

hē was wet and cōld.
hē was wet and cold.
hē was wet and cold.
hē was wet and cold.

a	a a a	d	d d d
b	b b b	e	e e e
c	c c c	f	f f f

1. jill's sister did not .

   • crȳ   • trēē   (• trȳ)

2. jill said, "if you trȳ, you will not
   have to ."

   • trȳ   (• crȳ)   • trēē

---

1. māke <u>t</u> in the box.

2. māke <u>c</u> in the circle.

[box with †]   [circle with c]

1. hē has some **fish**____.

2. that **rat**____ is fat.

---

shē was nāmed Jill.

shē was named Jill.

shē was named Jill.

10

1. dĭd Jill trȳ to do thiñgs?

   (• yes)   • nō

2. dĭd her sister trȳ to do thiñgs?

   • yes   (• nō)

3. can her sister rēad books?

   • yes   (• nō)

---

1. māke <u>r</u> in the circle.

2. māke <u>d</u> in the box.

[circle with r]   [box with d]

1. they are in a **lake**____

2. the girl is gōiñg
   after the **fish**____.

---

dĭd her sister trȳ?

dĭd her sister trȳ?

dĭd her sister trȳ?

---

the girl got a pot. then shē got a fish.
shē said, "this fish will gō in the pot."

1. the got a pot.

   • man   • boy   (• girl)

2. shē said, "this ____ will gō in the pot."

   • fan   (• fish)   • flȳ

---

mom had lots of cars. shē had a red car.
shē had nīne whīte cars.

1. ____ had lots of cars.

   • man   • men   (• mom)

2. shē had nīne ____ cars.

   • back   (• whīte)   • big

---

k	<u>k</u>	<u>k</u>	<u>k</u>	f	<u>f</u>	<u>f</u>	<u>f</u>
u	<u>u</u>	<u>u</u>	<u>u</u>	y	<u>y</u>	<u>y</u>	<u>y</u>
z	<u>z</u>	<u>z</u>	<u>z</u>	r	<u>r</u>	<u>r</u>	<u>r</u>

---

a boy did not talk to girls. hē talked
to cows. hē talked to gōats.

1. a boy did not talk to ____.

   • gātes   (• girls)   • cats

2. hē ____ to gōats.

   • walked   (• talked)   • said

---

the rabbit went down a slīde. shē went
on her nōse. her nōse was sōre.

1. the ____ went down a slīde.

   • ram   • rat   (• rabbit)

2. shē went on her ____.

   • sock   (• nōse)   • rōse

---

p	<u>p</u>	<u>p</u>	<u>p</u>	f	<u>f</u>	<u>f</u>	<u>f</u>
d	<u>d</u>	<u>d</u>	<u>d</u>	g	<u>g</u>	<u>g</u>	<u>g</u>
b	<u>b</u>	<u>b</u>	<u>b</u>	c	<u>c</u>	<u>c</u>	<u>c</u>

1. Jon was gōīng to bāke a ▦▦▦ cāke.
   • big   • cat   ⬭ fish

2. did his sister help him?
   • yes   ⬭ nō

3. did his mother help him?
   • yes   ⬭ nō

___

1. māke _s_ in the circle.
2. māke _r_ in the box.

Ⓢ [r]

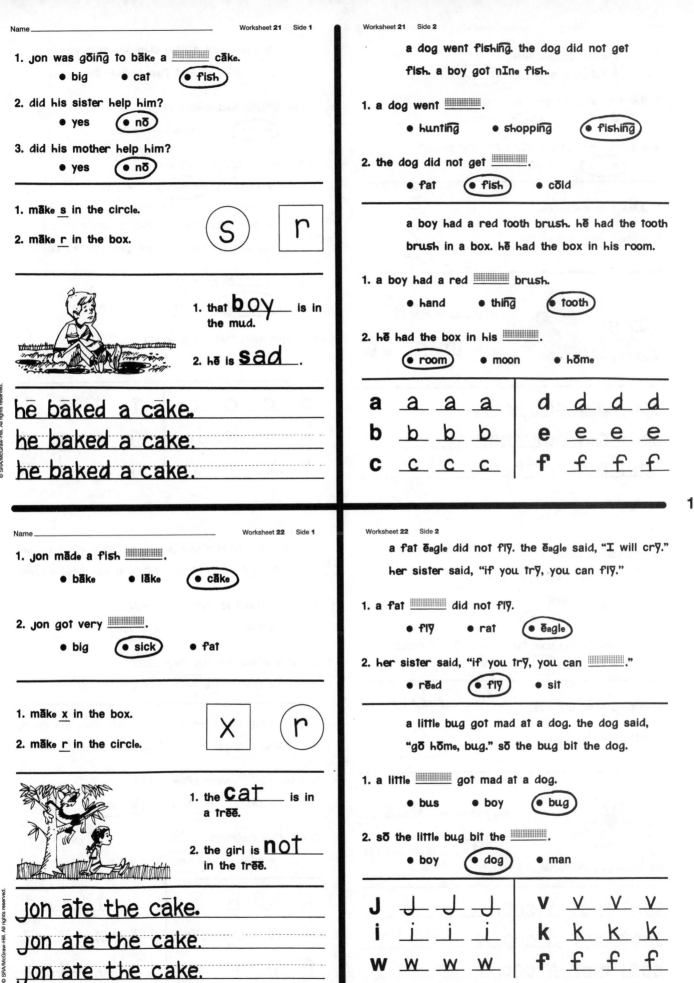

1. that **boy** is in the mud.

2. hē is **sad** .

hē bāked a cāke.
he baked a cake.
he baked a cake.

a dog went fīshǐng. the dog did not get fish. a boy got nīne fish.

1. a dog went ▦▦▦.
   • hunting   • shopping   ⬭ fishing

2. the dog did not get ▦▦▦.
   • fat   ⬭ fish   • cōld

___

a boy had a red tooth brush. hē had the tooth brush in a box. hē had the box in his room.

1. a boy had a red ▦▦▦ brush.
   • hand   • thing   ⬭ tooth

2. hē had the box in his ▦▦▦.
   ⬭ room   • moon   • hōme

a	a̲	a̲	a̲	d	d̲	d̲	d̲
b	b̲	b̲	b̲	e	e̲	e̲	e̲
c	c̲	c̲	c̲	f	f̲	f̲	f̲

11

1. Jon māde a fish ▦▦▦.
   • bāke   • lāke   ⬭ cāke

2. Jon got very ▦▦▦.
   • big   ⬭ sick   • fat

___

1. māke _x_ in the box.
2. māke _r_ in the circle.

[X] Ⓡ

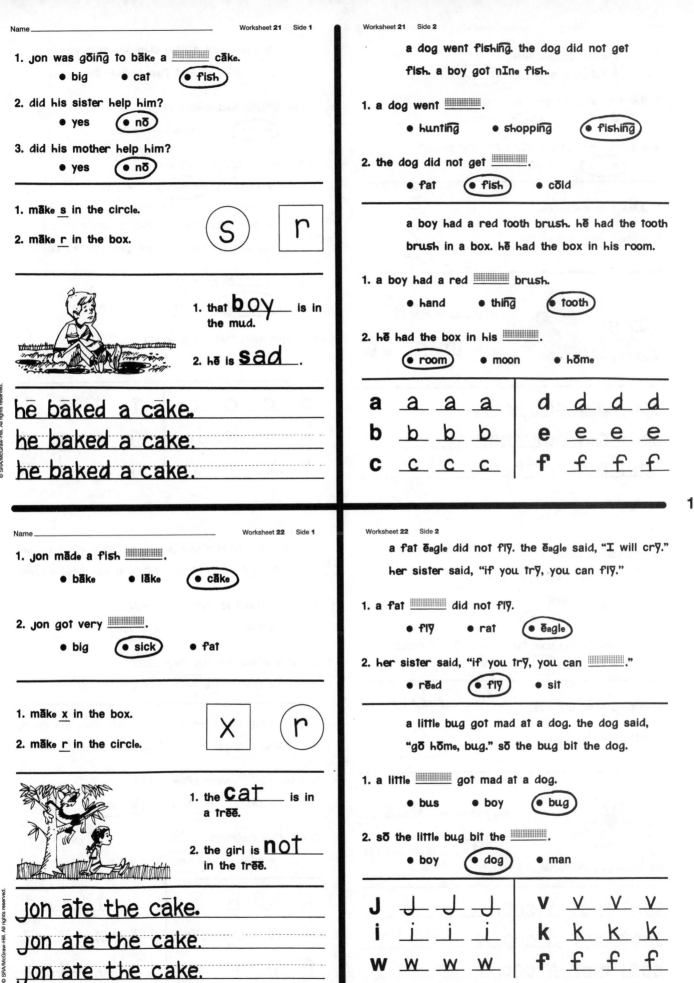

1. the **cat** is in a trēē.

2. the girl is **not** in the trēē.

Jon āte the cāke.
Jon ate the cake.
Jon ate the cake.

a fat ēagle did not flȳ. the ēagle said, "I will crȳ." her sister said, "if you trȳ, you can flȳ."

1. a fat ▦▦▦ did not flȳ.
   • flȳ   • rat   ⬭ ēagle

2. her sister said, "if you trȳ, you can ▦▦▦."
   • rēad   ⬭ flȳ   • sit

___

a little bug got mad at a dog. the dog said, "gō hōme, bug." sō the bug bit the dog.

1. a little ▦▦▦ got mad at a dog.
   • bus   • boy   ⬭ bug

2. sō the little bug bit the ▦▦▦.
   • boy   ⬭ dog   • man

J	J̲	J̲	J̲	v	v̲	v̲	v̲
i	i̲	i̲	i̲	k	k̲	k̲	k̲
w	w̲	w̲	w̲	f	f̲	f̲	f̲

1. spot did not ▨▨▨▨ well.
  ● ēat   ● ēar   (● hēar)

2. the man in the stōre said, "give mē a ▨▨▨▨."
  ● lot   (● dIme)   ● bit

3. did spot give him a dIme fōr the bōnes?
  (● yes)   ● nō

---

1. māke z in the circle.

2. māke s ōver the circle.

S
(Z)

---

1. shē is in a **car** ___.

2. the **man** ___ is big.

---

spot did not hēar.
spot did not hear.
spot did not hear.

12

the boy had a little ship. his ship was
on a lāke. hē had fun in that ship.

1. the ▨▨▨▨ had a little ship.
  (● boy)   ● bus   ● toy

2. hē had ▨▨▨▨ in that ship.
  ● sand   (● fun)   ● fish

---

a duck walked on a rōad. a man cāme up in
his car. hē said, "let mē give you a rIde."

1. a duck ▨▨▨▨ on a rōad.
  (● walked)   ● jumped   ● talked

2. a man said, "let mē give you a ▨▨▨▨."
  ● duck   ● rōad   (● rIde)

---

c	c c c	t	t t t
k	k k k	g	g g g
v	v v v	d	d d d

---

1. was spot a cat?
  ● yes   (● nō)

2. did spot hēar well?
  ● yes   (● nō)

3. spot said to the cop, "you are a ▨▨▨▨ cop."
  ● fat   (● good)   ● bad

---

1. māke b ōver the box.

2. māke c in the box.

b
C

---

1. the cat is on a **box** ___.

2. a **rat** ___ is on the cat.

---

spot met a cop.
spot met a cop.
spot met a cop.

sal lIked to run and jump. but shē did not lIke
to ēat. wē said, "if you ēat, you can rēad a book."

1. ▨▨▨▨ lIked to run and jump.
  ● sat   ● sad   (● sal)

2. but shē did not lIke to ▨▨▨▨.
  ● talk   (● ēat)   ● ēar

---

a big shark went after a little fish. the shark
did not get the fish. the fish swam too fast.

1. a big ▨▨▨▨ went after a little fish.
  ● cat   ● hōrse   (● shark)

2. the fish swam too ▨▨▨▨.
  ● slōw   (● fast)   ● fat

---

h	h h h	t	t t t
m	m m m	z	z z z
p	p p p	Y	Y Y Y

1. dōn līked to ask ░░░░░.
   - what   - when   (- why)

2. don dug a hōle in the ░░░░░.
   (- yard)   - farm   - car

3. don got a can of ░░░░░ pāint.
   - what   (- whīte)   - why

---

1. māke x in the circle.

2. māke m ōver the circle.

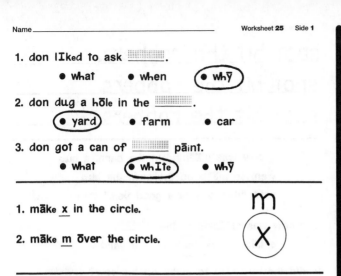

1. the girl has a **fish** .
2. the boy has a **hat** .

---

hē dug a big hōle.
he dug a big hole.
he dug a big hole.

sid was a fat dog. sid walked and
walked. but sid did not run fast.

1. ░░░░░ was a fat dog.
   - sam   (- sid)   - sad

2. but sid did not ░░░░░ fast.
   - talk   - jump   (- run)

---

nell was a whīte hōrse. shē ran in
the rāin. shē ran as fast as a dēēr.

1. ░░░░░ was a whīte hōrse.
   - bill   - fill   (- nell)

2. shē ░░░░░ as fast as a dēēr.
   (- ran)   - slid   - jumps

---

y	y̶ y̶ y̶	c	c c c
v	v v v	g	g̶ g̶ g̶
w	w w w	f	f f f

13

---

1. what did don līke to ask?
   (- why)   - when   - where

2. who asked him what hē was doing with his bīke?
   - his brother   - his mother   (- his sister)

---

1. māke m in the circle.

2. māke a ōver the circle.

3. māke r under the circle.

a
m
r

---

1. māke t ōver the box.

2. māke s under the box.

3. māke a in the box.

t
a
s

dōn pāinted and pāinted.
don painted and painted.
don painted and painted.

---

sam went fishing at the lāke. hē was
at the lāke fōr a little tIme. hē cāme
back with fIve fish.

1. sam went ░░░░░ at the lāke.
   - swimming   - hunting   (- fishing)

2. hē cāme back with ░░░░░ fish.
   (- fIve)   - big   - nIne

---

spot līked to ēat mēat.
and spot āte bōnes.
spot had a lot of bōnes.

1. ░░░░░ līked to ēat mēat.
   - pot   (- spot)   - stop

2. spot had a ░░░░░ of bōnes.
   - room   - tub   (- lot)

1. the robbers cāme from the stōre with ▨▨▨.
   - • bags of toys
   - • (bags of monēy)
   - • bags of dīmes

2. the robbers had a big ▨▨▨.
   - • ēar
   - • bag
   - • (hōrn)

3. spot bit the robbers on the ▨▨▨.
   - • (legs)
   - • ēars
   - • nōse

4. was the cop happy?
   - • (yes)
   - • nō

---

1. māke t in the circle.
2. māke s ōver the box.
3. māke m in the box.

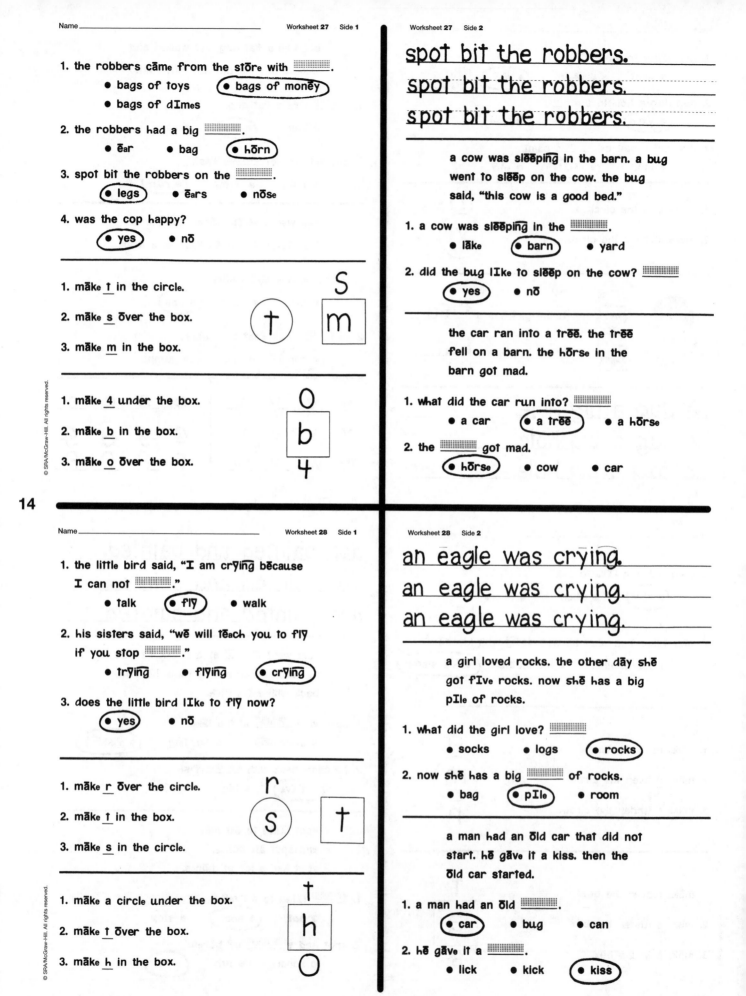

S

† m

---

1. māke 4 under the box.
2. māke b in the box.
3. māke o ōver the box.

0

b

4

14

spot bit the robbers.
spot bit the robbers.
spot bit the robbers.

a cow was slēēpīng in the barn. a bug
went to slēēp on the cow. the bug
said, "this cow is a good bed."

1. a cow was slēēpīng in the ▨▨▨.
   - • lāke
   - • (barn)
   - • yard

2. did the bug līke to slēēp on the cow? ▨▨▨
   - • (yes)
   - • nō

---

the car ran into a trēē. the trēē
fell on a barn. the hōrse in the
barn got mad.

1. what did the car run into? ▨▨▨
   - • a car
   - • (a trēē)
   - • a hōrse

2. the ▨▨▨ got mad.
   - • (hōrse)
   - • cow
   - • car

---

1. the little bird said, "I am crȳīng bēcause
   I can not ▨▨▨."
   - • talk
   - • (flȳ)
   - • walk

2. his sisters said, "wē will tēach you to flȳ
   if you stop ▨▨▨."
   - • trȳīng
   - • flȳīng
   - • (crȳīng)

3. does the little bird līke to flȳ now?
   - • (yes)
   - • nō

---

1. māke r ōver the circle.
2. māke t in the box.
3. māke s in the circle.

r

s † t

---

1. māke a circle under the box.
2. māke t ōver the box.
3. māke h in the box.

† t

h

O

an eagle was crȳīng.
an eagle was crying.
an eagle was crying.

a girl loved rocks. the other dāy shē
got fīve rocks. now shē has a big
pīle of rocks.

1. what did the girl love? ▨▨▨
   - • socks
   - • logs
   - • (rocks)

2. now shē has a big ▨▨▨ of rocks.
   - • bag
   - • (pīle)
   - • room

---

a man had an ōld car that did not
start. hē gāve it a kiss. then the
ōld car started.

1. a man had an ōld ▨▨▨.
   - • (car)
   - • bug
   - • can

2. hē gāve it a ▨▨▨.
   - • lick
   - • kick
   - • (kiss)

1. the farmer had his best buttons on his ▦▦▦.

   • hat   • socks   (• pants)

2. a man cãme to the farm to ▦▦▦.

   • sēē buttons   • sell buttons

   (• buy buttons)

3. did the farmer sell some of his buttons?

   (• yes)   • no

---

1. mãke i in the box.

2. mãke c under the box.

3. mãke b ōver the circle.

b

i

c

---

1. mãke r in the circle.

2. mãke a box ōver the circle.

3. mãke 6 under the circle.

r

6

that farmer had buttons.
that farmer had buttons.
that farmer had buttons.

---

jill went fishĩng and got fIve fish.
she ran awãy when a fox cãme nēar.
the fox ãte her fish.

1. jill went ▦▦▦.

   • diggĩng   • swimmĩng   (• fishĩng)

2. the ▦▦▦ ãte her fish.

   • box   (• fox)   • for

---

mother gãve pam some gōld. when pam cãme
back, she said, "I sōld the gōld so that I can
get a bIke." now pam has a red bIke.

1. what did mother give to pam? ▦▦▦

   • a bIke   (• some gōld)   • a hōld

2. what did pam get? ▦▦▦

   (• a bIke)   • some gōld   • a sack

15

1. the farmer sōld the buttons that held up ▦▦▦.

   • his hat   (• his pants)   • his cōat

2. then his pants ▦▦▦.

   • held up   • had buttons   (• fell down)

3. now the farmer has monēy, but he has no
   ▦▦▦.

   • pants   • socks   (• buttons)

---

1. mãke a circle next to the box.

2. mãke t in the circle.

3. mãke s in the box.

t

s

---

1. mãke e under the circle.

2. mãke 5 ōver the box.

3. mãke t in the box.

5

t

e

he sōld his buttons.
he sold his buttons.
he sold his buttons.

---

her mom gãve her a kiss. so she gãve
her dog a kiss. then the dog gãve
the cat a kiss.

1. what did her mom give her? ▦▦▦

   • a kick   • a card   (• a kiss)

2. the dog kissed the ▦▦▦.

   • mom   (• cat)   • dog

---

a big tIger met a little tIger. the
big tIger said, "let's ēat." so the
little tIger ãte the big tIger.

1. the big tIger said, "▦▦▦."

   (• let's ēat)   • let's go   • let's talk

2. what did the little tIger ēat? ▦▦▦

   • the little tIger   (• the big tIger)   • cōrn

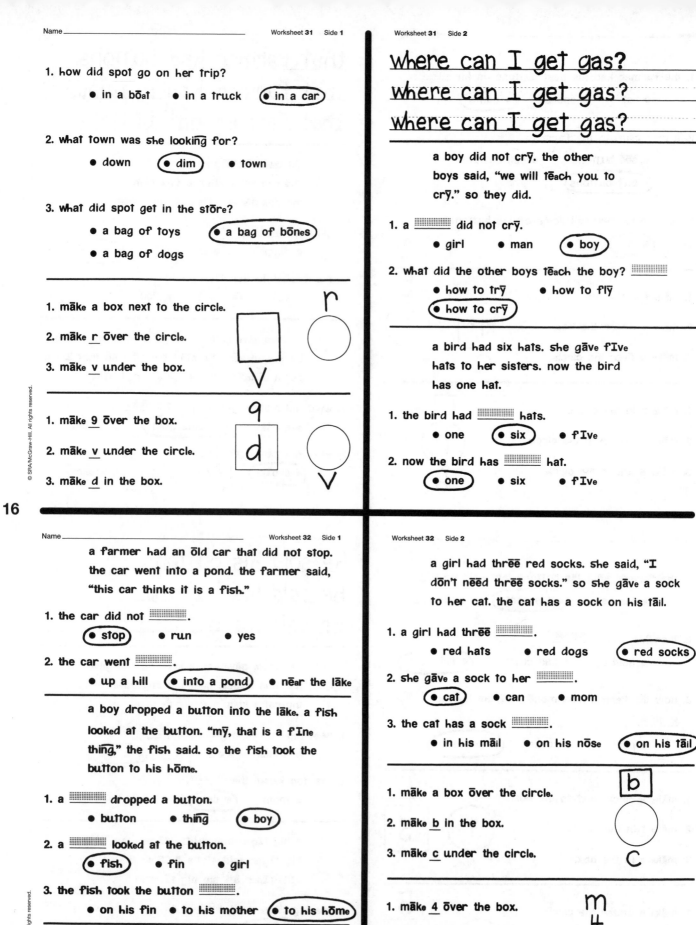

1. how did spot go on her trip?

   • in a bōat   • in a truck   (• in a car)

2. what town was she looking for?

   • down   (• dim)   • town

3. what did spot get in the stōre?

   • a bag of toys   (• a bag of bōnes)

   • a bag of dogs

___

1. māke a box next to the circle.

2. māke _r_ ōver the circle.

3. māke _v_ under the box.

1. māke _9_ ōver the box.

2. māke _v_ under the circle.

3. māke _d_ in the box.

where can I get gas?
where can I get gas?
where can I get gas?

a boy did not crȳ. the other
boys said, "we will tēach you to
crȳ." so they did.

1. a ▨▨▨▨ did not crȳ.

   • girl   • man   (• boy)

2. what did the other boys tēach the boy? ▨▨▨▨

   • how to trȳ   • how to flȳ

   (• how to crȳ)

___

a bird had six hats. she gāve fīve
hats to her sisters. now the bird
has one hat.

1. the bird had ▨▨▨▨ hats.

   • one   (• six)   • fīve

2. now the bird has ▨▨▨▨ hat.

   (• one)   • six   • fīve

16

a farmer had an ōld car that did not stop.
the car went into a pond. the farmer said,
"this car thinks it is a fish."

1. the car did not ▨▨▨▨.

   (• stop)   • run   • yes

2. the car went ▨▨▨▨.

   • up a hill   (• into a pond)   • nēar the lāke

___

a boy dropped a button into the lāke. a fish
looked at the button. "mȳ, that is a fīne
thing," the fish said. so the fish took the
button to his hōme.

1. a ▨▨▨▨ dropped a button.

   • button   • thing   (• boy)

2. a ▨▨▨▨ looked at the button.

   (• fish)   • fin   • girl

3. the fish took the button ▨▨▨▨.

   • on his fin   • to his mother   (• to his hōme)

___

will she stāy at hōme?
will she stay at home?

a girl had thrēe red socks. she said, "I
dōn't nēed thrēe socks." so she gāve a sock
to her cat. the cat has a sock on his tāil.

1. a girl had thrēe ▨▨▨▨.

   • red hats   • red dogs   (• red socks)

2. she gāve a sock to her ▨▨▨▨.

   (• cat)   • can   • mom

3. the cat has a sock ▨▨▨▨.

   • in his māil   • on his nōse   (• on his tāil)

___

1. māke a box ōver the circle.

2. māke _b_ in the box.

3. māke _c_ under the circle.

___

1. māke _4_ ōver the box.

2. māke _m_ ōver the _4_.

3. māke _6_ in the circle.

1. whȧt did this dog līke to do?
- walk, walk, walk
- tāke, tāke, tāke
- (talk, talk, talk)

2. did the dog līke to plāy ball?
- yes
- (no)

3. so the man got very ░░░░░.
- (mad)
- sad
- ōld

---

1. māke a circle next to the box.

2. māke a under the box.

3. māke e in the circle.

(e)   [a]

1. māke g in the circle.

2. māke n ōver the circle.

3. māke o under the box.

n
(g)   [o]

a boy loved to rīde cows. his dad said,
"why do you rīde a cow when you have a
hōrse?"
so now the hōrse rīdes the cow.

1. whȧt did the boy love to rīde? ░░░░░
- dogs
- (cows)
- hōrses

2. a ░░░░░ rīdes the cow now.
- (hōrse)
- boy
- cow

---

a girl had nīne buttons on her hat. her mom
gāve her another button. now the girl has ten
buttons on her hat.

1. whȧt did her mom give her? ░░░░░
- nīne buttons
- (another button)
- ten buttons

2. she has ░░░░░ buttons now.
- nīne
- one
- (ten)

---

she can rēad, rēad, rēad.
she can read, read, read.
she can read, read, read.

1. the small bug did not have a ░░░░░.
- sister
- (hōme)
- hōle

2. wher̄e did he trȳ to live?
- in a cup
- in a shack
- (in a stall)

3. at last he cāme to a ░░░░░.
- (ball)
- town
- man

4. did the bug līke the ball?
- (yes)
- no

---

1. māke a box ōver the circle.

2. māke d ōver the box.

3. māke m under the circle.

d
[□]
○
m

1. māke a 6 in the circle.

2. māke a 3 under the box.

3. māke h ōver the box.

h
(6)   [   ]
3

a man cāme to the farm. he said,
"I want to buȳ some cows."
so the farmer sōld him six cows.

1. whȧt did the man want? ░░░░░
- farms
- men
- (cows)

2. the farmer sōld ░░░░░ cows.
- (six)
- fīve
- no

---

a girl got mad at her dog for digging
hōles. her dog dug up gōld.
now the girl is not mad.

1. her dog ░░░░░ up gōld.
- (dug)
- man
- bug

2. the girl is not ░░░░░ now.
- had
- mud
- (mad)

---

he went into the ball.
he went into the ball.
he went into the ball.

1. the bug went to sleep in the ░░░░░.
   - hall   - (ball)   - bed

2. when he woke up, the ball was ░░░░░.
   - running   - (rolling)   - walking

3. what did the girl say to the bug?
   - "I love bugs."   - "I eat bugs."
   - ("I hate bugs.")

---

1. make a circle over the box.

2. make u under the box.

3. make s over the circle.

s
◯
▢
u

---

1. make k under the circle.

2. make s over the box.

3. make a 2 in the circle.

② k

S
▢

18

a farmer was mad at a bug. "stop eating my corn," the farmer said. so the bug stopped eating corn and ate the farmer's hat.

1. a ░░░░░ was mad.
   - bug   - (farmer)   - girl

2. the farmer said, "stop eating my ░░░░░."
   - farm   - hat   - (corn)

---

an eagle fell from a tree.
he fell on a dog.
the dog started to cry.

1. an eagle fell on a ░░░░░.
   - (dog)   - tree   - eagle

2. what did the dog start to do? ░░░░░
   - (cry)   - run   - bark

---

this ball is my home.
this ball is my home.
this ball is my home.

---

1. the small bug wanted to ░░░░░ in the ball.
   - look   - (stay)   - run

2. the bug said, "I will ░░░░░ with you."
   - (play)   - stay   - sit

3. did the girl want to come to the party?
   - yes   - (no)

---

1. make a circle over the box.

2. make s in the box.

3. make r over the circle.

r
◯
▢
S

---

1. make qu in the box.

2. make b under the circle.

3. make a 7 over the box.

7
▢
qu   ◯

b

a shark met a cat. the shark said, "get on my back and go for a rIde." so the cat got on the shark's back and went for a rIde.

1. the cat got on the shark's ░░░░░.
   - nose   - (back)   - fin

2. where did the cat go? ░░░░░
   - (for a rIde)   - for a cop   - for a shark

---

a boy asked spot, "why is your nose cold?" spot said, "so you can feel it when I kiss you." then she gave the boy a kiss.

1. spot had a cold ░░░░░.
   - tail   - (nose)   - ear

2. what did she give the boy? ░░░░░
   - a nose   - a cold   - (a kiss)

---

please let me stay.
please let me stay.
please let me stay.

1. a tall girl wanted the bug to fīnd ▓▓▓.
   - a hōrse   • another hōme
   - another barn

2. her ▓▓▓ cāme into the room.
   - brother   • sister   • mother

3. the girl māde a ▓▓▓ with her brother.
   - bad   • wish   • bet

---

1. māke a box next to the circle.

2. māke <u>m</u> in the box.

3. māke <u>r</u> ōver the circle.

---

1. māke an <u>8</u> under the box.

2. māke <u>y</u> ōver the box.

3. māke <u>p</u> in the circle.

a man was gōīng on a trip. there was
room in his car for a bīke and a dog.
but then there was no room for the man.

1. the man was gōīng on a ▓▓▓.
   - bīke   • dog   • trip

2. there was no room for the ▓▓▓.
   - man   • dog   • car

---

ron asked a fish, "what do you līke
to ēat?" the fish said, "I love bugs."
so ron gāve the fish a big bug.

1. what did the fish līke to ēat? ▓▓▓
   - cats   • fish   • bugs

2. what did ron give the fish? ▓▓▓
   - a big bar   • a big bug   • a little bug

I will tāke that bet.
I will take that bet.
I will take that bet.

19

---

1. did the brother sēē the bug in the ball?
   - yes   • no

2. whȳ did the ball start to rōll?
   - the bug crīed.   • the brother bet.
   - the bug ran.

3. how did the stōry end?
   - the bug stopped.   • the bug stāyed.
   - the bug went far.

---

1. māke a box under the circle.

2. māke <u>t</u> under the box.

3. māke <u>b</u> under the t.

---

1. māke a <u>4</u> in the box.

2. māke <u>c</u> in the circle.

3. māke <u>t</u> ōver the circle.

fīve dogs dug a hōle to look for bōnes.
they saw gōld in the hōle.
dogs cannot ēat gōld, so the dogs got mad.

1. fīve dogs dug a ▓▓▓.
   - bōnes   • hōle   • gōld

2. what can't dogs ēat? ▓▓▓
   - gōld   • mēat   • ham

---

there was a cat that loved to ēat, ēat, ēat,
so she sat on her sēat, sēat, sēat, and she
āte lots of mēat, mēat, mēat,

1. what did the cat love to do? ▓▓▓
   - hit   • ēat   • mēat

2. what did she ēat? ▓▓▓
   - mēat   • ēat   • bēans

---

māke that ball rōll.
make that ball roll.
make that ball roll.

1. a small elephant always ▨▨▨.
   - • jumped down   • sat down   • **fell down**

2. the elephant said, "I ▨▨▨ to fall."
   - • lIke   • **hāte**   • want

3. a tall girl gāve him ▨▨▨.
   - • some fish   • some grass   • **some glasses**

4. was the elephant happy at the end of the stōry?
   - **yes**   • no

---

1. māke a circle ōver the box.

2. māke g ōver the circle.

3. māke s ōver the g.

1. māke y under the circle.

2. māke a 9 under the box.

3. māke a ōver the box.

spot had a dIme. the man at the stōre said,
"you can get some bōnes for that dIme."
spot said, "no, I want some ham."

1. spot had a ▨▨▨.
   - • **dIme**   • bōne   • stōre

2. what did spot want? ▨▨▨
   - • some bōnes   • **some ham**   • some dImes

---

sam māde a mud cāke.
he āte the cāke by him self.
the cāke māde him sick.

1. what did sam māke? ▨▨▨
   - • a mud lāke   • a fish cāke   • **a mud cāke**

2. he āte the cāke ▨▨▨.
   - **by him self**   • in his room   • in the yard

---

do you need glasses?
do you need glasses?
do you need glasses?

20

---

1. the dog ▨▨▨ to rēad books.
   - • hāted   • **loved**   • trIed

2. what was the tall man looking for?
   - • his hat   • his ball   • **his book**

3. why was the tall man mad at the dog?
   - **the dog took his book.**
   - • the dog took his ball.
   - • the dog took his hat.

4. the dog hid the book when the tall man was ▨▨▨.
   - • in the room   • **in the hall**   • sleēping

---

1. māke the word sun in the circle.

2. māke the word cat under the circle.

1. māke a box next to the circle.

2. māke r in the box.

3. māke b under the circle.

pam had ten footballs. she gāve her sister
one football. now pam has nIne footballs.

1. what did pam have? ▨▨▨
   - • ten sisters   • one football
   - **ten footballs**

2. how many footballs did she give to her sister? ▨▨▨
   - • six   • seven   • **one**

---

a small cat had a ham. a big cat said, "give
me a bIte." so the small cat bit the big cat.

1. what did the small cat have? ▨▨▨
   - **a ham**   • a hat   • a home

2. the big cat said, "▨▨▨."
   - • give me a bit   • **give me a bIte**
   - • give me a ham

---

will you plāy ball?
will you play ball?
will you play ball?

1. did walter plăy football well?
   - yes
   - (no)

2. when walter ran to get a pass, he ░░░░░.
   - kicked the football
   - (dropped the football)
   - held the football

3. the other boys tōld him, "you ░░░ drop the football."
   - also
   - never
   - (always)

4. walter was a very ░░░ boy.
   - (sad)
   - mĕan
   - glad

---

1. māke the word <u>log</u> under the circle.

2. māke the word <u>fat</u> in the box.

fat

log

---

1. māke <u>p</u> ōver the box.

2. māke <u>j</u> ōver the <u>p</u>.

3. māke <u>h</u> under the box.

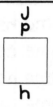

J
P

h

a bird said, "I cannot flȳ."
the bird's brother said, "I will shōw you
how to flȳ." so the bird and his brother
went to an ēagle.

1. a bird said, "░░░."
   - I will not flȳ
   - (I cannot flȳ)
   - you do not trȳ

2. where did the bird and his brother go?
   - to a farm
   - to a rabbit
   - (to an ēagle)

---

a girl had six cows. she găve three cows to
her dad. now the girl has three cows.

1. how many cows did the girl give to her dad?
   - one
   - six
   - (three)

2. how many cows does she have now?
   - one
   - (three)
   - six

---

why do you always fall?
why do you always fall?
why do you always fall?
why do you always fall?

1. there was a big football ░░░.
   - nāme
   - (gāme)
   - plăy

2. where was the gāme plăyed?
   - (in a lot)
   - in a stōre
   - in a room

3. was walter plăyĭng on his tēam?
   - yes
   - (no)

4. walter said, "that other tēam is gōĭng to ░░░."
   - wish
   - walk
   - (win)

5. walter said, "I ░░░ I could help mȳ tēam."
   - walk
   - (wish)
   - went

---

1. māke <u>h</u> next to the box.

2. māke <u>k</u> ōver the box.

3. māke <u>f</u> ōver the <u>h</u>.

f
h

k

---

1. māke the word <u>it</u> under the box.

2. māke the word <u>so</u> ōver the circle.

so

it

fīve men took gōld from a stōre. a cop
stopped them. now the men have no gōld.

1. where did the men get the gōld?
   - from a cop
   - from a jāil
   - (from a stōre)

2. what do the men have now?
   - a cop
   - (no gōld)
   - some gōld

---

jill's sister said, "I cannot rēad. but I will
trȳ." the next dāy, she said, "I cannot rēad.
but I will trȳ." she kept trȳĭng and now she
is rēadĭng.

1. what did jill's sister sāy?
   - (I will trȳ.)
   - I will crȳ.
   - I will flȳ.

2. what can jill's sister do now?
   - crȳ
   - (rēad)
   - rōad

---

how could they win?
how could they win?
how could they win?
how could they win?

1. the other tēam had two ▨▨▨▨.
   • balls   • boys   (• scōres)

2. the ▨▨▨▨ plāyer on walter's tēam cut his arm.
   • big   (• best)   • tall

3. did the tēam ask walter to plāy?
   (• yes)   • no

4. whȳ did they ask walter?
   • they nēēded a ball.   • they nēēded a plāy.
   (• they nēēded a plāyer.)

1. māke _b_ next to the circle.

2. māke _t_ under the circle.

3. māke _s_ under the _b_.

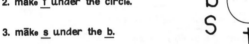

1. māke the word _mad_ in the box.

2. māke the word _sad_ in the circle.

jāne said, "I can plāy football better than any boy."
the boys said, "hō, hō." but jāne was the best plāyer in the gāme.

1. what did the boys sāy?
   • "oh, no"   • "no, no"   (• "hō, hō")

2. did jāne plāy well?
   (• yes)   • no

the talking dog said, "I will go in the hall, hall, hall." so he went to the hall. then he said, "I will plāy some ball, ball, ball." so he did.

1. where did the dog go?
   • to a ball   (• to the hall)   • to a wall

2. what did he do?
   (• plāyed ball)   • called   • āte salt

"come hēre," they called.
"come hēre," they called.
"come hēre," they called.
"come hēre," they called.

22

1. walter's tēam was gōing to ▨▨▨▨.
   (• kick the ball)   • pass the ball   • run the ball

2. did the other boys think that they could kick the ball that far?
   • yes   (• no)

3. walter said, "I ▨▨▨▨ I could kick the ball that far."
   • thank   (• think)   • plāyer

4. walter said to himself, "I will not ▨▨▨▨."
   (• fall)   • kick   • run

1. māke _b_ ōver the box.

2. māke _r_ next to the _b_.

3. māke _s_ ōver the _b_.

1. māke the word _fox_ under the circle.

2. māke the word _flȳ_ in the box.

jāne did not līke fish. so she gāve her fish to her dog. the dog said, "it is fun to ēat fish."

1. what didn't jāne līke?
   • dogs   (• fish)   • cāke

2. what did she do with her fish?
   (• gāve it to her dog)   • āte it   • sat on it

thrēē bugs wanted to plāy football. the football was a sēed. they had a good gāme. but one bug āte the sēed. then the bugs had to stop plāying football.

1. how many bugs plāyed football?
   (• thrēē)   • one   • six

2. where is the sēed?
   • one bug cooked it.   (• one bug āte it.)
   • thrēē bugs āte it.

I will not fall.
I will not fall.
I will not fall.
I will not fall.

1. what did walter do in this story?

- ran with the ball   • picked up the ball

(• kicked the ball)

2. the ball went lIke a ▨▨▨▨▨.

- stop   • shop   (• shot)

3. they called, "that's the way to ▨▨▨▨▨."

- run   (• kick)   • shot

4. what did walter's team need to win?

(• one more score)   • one more boy

- one more ball

---

1. make _s_ next to the circle.

2. make _t_ over the _s_.

3. make _y_ under the _s_.

---

1. make the word _fun_ over the box.

2. make the word _box_ under the circle.

jan got in a tall tree. her mom said, "don't fall from that tall tree." jan did not fall from the tree. she jumped from the tree.

1. where did jan go?

(• in a tall tree)   • in a hall   • near a ball

2. how did jan get from the tall tree?

- she fell.   (• she jumped.)   • she ran.

---

a farmer got on a horse. the horse did not want to go. she wanted to eat. so the farmer gave the horse some seeds. she ate the seeds. then she and the farmer took a rIde.

1. what did the farmer give the horse?

- some weeds   • some kicks   (• some seeds)

2. what did the horse and the farmer do?

(• they took a rIde.)   • they started to cry.

---

he can kick the ball.
he can kick the ball.
he can kick the ball.
he can kick the ball.

23

---

1. walter said, "I think I can ▨▨▨▨▨ the ball all the way."

- run   (• kick)   • jump

2. did walter's team win the game?

(• yes)   • no

3. why was walter happy?

- because he ate candy

(• because he was the star of the game)

- because he hit the ball

4. can walter play football any tIme he wants?

(• yes)   • no

---

1. make a box over the circle.

2. make _t_ in the box.

3. make _n_ under the circle.

---

1. make the word _car_ in the box.

2. make the word _old_ under the box.

a cow did not go "moo." that cow went "arf, arf."
every tIme the cow went "arf, arf," the farmer said, "I think I hear a dog."

1. what did the cow say?

(• "arf, arf")   • "moo"   • "boo, hoo"

2. the farmer said, "I think I hear a ▨▨▨▨▨."

- cow   (• dog)   • cat

---

dan's mom said, "if you eat lots of meat, you will get tall." so dan ate and ate. but he did not get tall. he got fat.

1. what did his mom tell him to eat?

- goats   (• meat)   • corn

2. what did dan get?

- meat   • tall   (• fat)

---

walter was happy.
walter was happy.
walter was happy.
walter was happy.

jāne said, "I will kick the ball far."
tim said, "I will hōld the ball for you."
jāne kicked the ball. she kicked the ball
very far.

1. what did jāne want to kick? __the ball__
   ● the ball   ● the boy   ● the bōat
2. what did tim hōld? __the ball__
   ● the bōat   ● the boy   ● the ball
3. what did jāne kick? __the ball__
   ● the toy   ● the boy   ● the ball

_____

a girl went out for the running tēam.
the boys on the tēam said, "that girl thinks
she can run fast."
the girl ran faster than the boys. then she
said, "hō, hō."

1. the girl went out for the running __team__.
   ● nōse   ● fast   ● tēam
   | Also accept tēam **or** tēam. |
2. did the boys think she could run fast? __no__
   ● yes   ● no
3. who ran faster? __the girl__
   ● the boys   ● the girl   ● the tēam
4. what did the girl sāy after she ran? __ho ho__
   ● "he, he"   ● "ha, ha"   ● "hō, hō"
   | Also accept hō, hō. |

24

1. what is the nāme of the cow in this stōry?
   __carmen__
   ● walter   ● moo   ● carmen
2. carmen has a very __loud__ moo.
   ● loud   ● little   ● fast
3. where did the children go? __to the farm__
   ● to the stōre   ● to the farm   ● to the lot
4. they cāme to __pet__ cows.
   ● see   ● pet   ● hit
5. one chīld fell __in a hole__ .
   ● in a box   ● in a hōle   ● in a crēēk
   | Also accept hōle **or** hōle. |

| thrēē men sat in a (car). |

1. circle the word car.
2. māke a līne ōver the word men.

_____

| her nāme was nell. |

1. māke a līne under the word her.
2. māke a līne ōver the word nell.

rēad this sentence.

| the dog (was) fat. |

1. circle the word was.
2. māke a līne ōver the word the.

_____

rēad this sentence.

| a fish āte a (ball). |

1. māke a līne ōver the word fish.
2. circle the word ball.

_____

rēad this sentence.

| a (girl) had a red hat. |

1. māke a līne ōver the word red.
2. circle the word girl.

a little shark was trȳing to swim. a fish
cāme up and asked, "can I give you a hand?"
the shark said, "fish dōn't have hands.
they have fins."

1. the fish asked if he could give the
   shark a __hand__ .   ● hand   ● trick   ● fish
2. do fish have hands? __no__   ● yes   ● no

_____

six old men and one dog went to the
lāke. fīve men said, "we hāte to swim." so
they sat on the shōre.
the other old man said, "I love to swim."
so he went swimming. the dog went to slēēp.

1. how many men hāted to swim? __five__ (or 5)
   ● six   ● one   ● fīve
2. what did the dog do? __went to sleep__
   ● went swimming   ● went to slēēp
   ● went to a show | Also accept slēēp. |

_____

__they cāme to pet cows.__
__they cāme to pet cows.__
__they cāme to pet cows.__

1. carmen had a ___loud___ moo.
   • lēad   • lōad   • loud   • little

2. carmen sāved the ___girl___ who fell into the hōle.
   • cow   • girl   • tēacher   • boy

3. the little girl ___kissed___ the cow.
   • kicked   • licked   • hit   • kissed

4. carmen was happy bēcause she had a big, loud ___moo___.
   • cow   • moon   • mom   • moo

(are) you s̄ad?

1. māke a līne ōver the word s̄ad.

2. circle the word are.

a farmer had a cow that could not moo. his dog said, "I will tēach that cow to moo." so he bēgan to tēach the cow. now the cow does not moo. she barks līke a dog.

1. the cow could not ___moo___.

2. who said, "I will tēach that cow to moo"?
   ___a dog___

3. what does the cow do now?
   ___barks like a dog___
   • moos   • barks līke a shark
   • swims līke a dog   • barks līke a dog

---

1. māke _h_ in the circle.

2. māke the word _sat_ under the circle.

3. māke a _9_ next to the word _sat_.

(h)
sat 9

25

1. what did jill have in the box? ___a mouse___
   • a house   • a rat   • a mouse
   • thrēē rats

2. who did she shōw the mouse to? her ___mother___
   • mother   • brother   • sister   • mouse

3. her mother said, "you can't kēēp that mouse in this ___house___."
   • box   • yard   • house   • room

4. where did jill tāke the mouse?
   to ___the yard___
   • her room   • the stōre   • the house
   • the yard

5. who didn't līke the mouse? ___her mother___
   • bēcause   • her mother   • in the yard
   • she was happy.

---

s̄he was not (fat)

1. circle the word fat.

2. māke a līne ōver the word s̄he.

a mouse was very sad. that mouse said, "I will fēēl better if I ēat a lot."
so the mouse āte and āte. at last, the mouse was so fat that he could not lēave his house. then he said, "I am rēally a sad mouse now."

1. the mouse was very ___sad___.

2. so what did the mouse do? ___ate a lot___
   • āte a lot   • sat a lot
   • went to slēēp   • went to his house

3. did the mouse fēēl better when he was fat? ___no___

4. who said, "I am rēally a sad mouse now"?
   ___the mouse___

---

1. māke a _2_ ōver the box.

2. māke the word _ant_ in the box.

3. māke the word _pig_ ōver the _2_.

pig
2
┌─────┐
│ ant │
└─────┘

1. where did the little girl live?

near a tall mountain
- on a tall hill
- in a barn
- in the clouds
- near a tall mountain

2. what did the girl want to see?

the top of the mountain
- the top of the mountain
- because it was tall
- her mother
- the top of the clouds

3. who went with the girl up the sIde of the

mountain? **her hound**
- to see the top
- her hound
- her mother
- the mountain

4. the sIde of the mountain was very **steep** .
- tall
- small
- steep
- street

---

the dog (sat) near the road.

1. make a lIne over the word road.

2. make a lIne under the word near.

3. circle the word sat.

a man said, "I need a button for my coat." so the man went to a store. but he did not go to a button store. he went to a seed store. now he has a coat with a big seed on it.

1. who said, "I need a button for my coat"? **a man**

2. did the man go to a button store? **no**

3. what did he buy at the store? **a seed**

4. where is the seed? **on his coat**
- on his hat
- in his mouth
- on his coat
- on his house

---

1. make the word no over the circle.

2. make v in the box.

3. make the word if under the circle.

no

if

V

---

1. where did the girl live? **near the mountain**
- near a lake
- near a house
- near the mountain
- on the mountain

2. who told her not to go up the mountain?

her mother
- her hound
- because it was tall
- her mother
- her father

3. what did the girl see when she came out of

the clouds? **a funny house**
- a funny house
- her father
- her mother
- a loud sound

4. what did the girl hear? **a loud sound**
- a house
- her mother
- a loud sound
- a hound

(she) ran very fast.

1. circle the word she.

2. make a lIne under the word fast.

3. make a lIne over the word very.

a girl picked up a pouch. her dad asked her, "what is in that pouch?"

the girl said, "an ouch."

her dad said, "you are silly. let me see what is in that pouch."

he took the pouch and put his hand insIde. "ouch," he said. the girl had a fish hook in her pouch.

1. who had an ouch pouch? **a girl**

2. who wanted to see what was in the pouch? **her dad**

3. what made her dad say "ouch"?

a fish hook
- a fish fin
- a hound
- a fish hook
- a hooked fish

4. did her dad get an ouch from the pouch? **yes**

---

1. make a 7 in the circle.

2. make a 6 over the circle.

3. make a next to the 6.

6 a

⑦

Also accept a to left of 6.

1. what did the girl hear coming from the house?

<u>a loud sound</u>
- a hound • a mouse
- a loud house • a loud sound

2. who did the girl see inside the house?

<u>nobody</u>
- nobody • her father • a door • a hound

3. what did the door do after the girl was inside?

<u>slammed behind her</u>
- opened • slammed behind her
- in the house • broke

4. what was hanging on the wall? a <u>pouch</u>
- pooch • hound • couch • pouch

---

she (was) not [sad].

1. make a box around the word <u>sad</u>.

2. circle the word <u>was</u>.

3. make a line over the word <u>she</u>.

a cow was riding in a car. the car ran out of gas. the cow asked a man, "can you give me some gas?"

the man said, "I'll give you gas if you give me milk." now the car has gas and the man has milk.

1. the <u>cow</u> was riding in a car.
- man • cow • dog

2. the cow asked a man,

"can you give me <u>some gas</u>?"
- some money • some milk • some gas

3. the man wanted the cow to give him some <u>milk</u>.
- gas • milk • cakes

---

1. make the word <u>bed</u> in the circle.

2. make the word <u>men</u> under the circle.

3. make a <u>4</u> under the word <u>men</u>.

(bed)
men
4

---

1. why didn't the girl leave the house?

the <u>door did not open</u>.
- door was little • door did not open
- pouch was little

2. the girl asked, "is there somebody in that <u>pouch</u>?"
- pouch • door • yard • hound

3. who lived in the pouch? <u>an elf</u>
- a thousand years • the girl
- an elf • an oaf

4. how many years had he lived in the pouch?

<u>a thousand years</u>
- the elf • a thousand years
- five years • no years

5. the elf said, "if you let me out,

I will give you <u>the pouch</u>."
- a hound • the house
- a cloud • the pouch

---

the dog [sat] on her bed.

1. circle the word <u>on</u>.

2. make a line over the word <u>dog</u>.

3. make a box around the word <u>sat</u>.

jack had a hound. jack said, "we must make a house for this hound." so jack got some logs and some rope and some rocks. now the hound has a house. jack likes the hound house so much that he goes in there to sleep with his hound.

1. who had a hound? <u>jack</u>

2. who made the hound house? <u>jack</u>

3. jack made the house of logs and rope and <u>rocks</u>.

4. what does jack do in the hound house?

<u>sleeps with his hound</u>
- sits with his mouse • talks in the house
- sleeps with his hound

---

1. make a circle under the circle.

2. make a box over the box.

3. cross out the circles.

1. what was hanging on the wall insIde the house?

a _pouch_
   • hound   • trēē   • pouch   • pooch

2. what was insIde that pouch? _an elf_
   • a house   • an elf   • a hound   • an ēēl

3. what did the girl's dog sāy when the elf ran around

the room? "_OWWWWW_"
   • who   • now   • owwwww   • grrrr

4. what did the elf give the girl? _the pouch_
   • when he cāme out of the pouch
   • the pouch   • a kiss

5. he tōld her, "when you are good, the pouch

will be _good_."
   • fat   • bad   • sick   • good

○	□
whȳ are you crȳing?	

1. māke a circle ōver the word whȳ.

2. māke a box ōver the word you.

3. māke a lIne under the word are.

28

a bug and a dog sat bȳ the sIde of the rōad. the bug said, "I do not lIke to walk. how can I get to the lāke?"

the dog said, "hop on mȳ back. I will tāke you to the lāke." so the dog took the bug to the lāke.

1. who sat bȳ the sIde of the rōad?

a _bug_ and a _dog_

2. did the bug lIke to walk? _no_

3. where did the bug want to go?

to the lake
   • to the ship   • to the log   • to the lāke

4. who took the bug to the lāke? _the dog_

---

1. māke a _b_ ōver the box.

2. māke the word ōver under the box.

3. māke the word under ōver the circle.

b   under

[square labeled "over"]   [circle]

---

1. the elf tōld the girl, "when you are good,

the pouch will be _good_."

2. "when you are bad, the _pouch_ will be _bad_."

3. what did the girl fInd in the pouch? _gold_
   • a sock   • good   • gōld   • a gōat

4. whȳ was the pouch good to her?

because she was good
   • after she was bad   • bēcause he was bad
   • bēcause she was good

5. the girl shouted, "I'm _rich_."
   • sick   • fat   • gōld   • rich

6. the girl and her hound started

down the _mountain_.
   • house   • pouch   • mountain   • clouds

7. when they rēached the bottom of the mountain,

it was _late_.
   • hot   • sun   • cōld   • lāte

8. the girl tōld her mother that she

went _to sleep_.
   • to slēēp   • to lIe
   • up the mountain   • to the stōre

○	
we want to ēat fish cāke.	
□	

1. māke a circle ōver the word want.

2. māke a box under the word want.

3. māke a lIne under the word fish.

---

pat said, "I want to go to the moon."

sal said, "moon girls have red hats. so I will māke you a red hat." sal got a can of red pāint and māde pat a red hat. sal said, "now you can go to the moon."

1. who wanted to go to the moon? _pat_
   • sal   • the moon girls   • pat

2. sal said, "moon girls have red _hats_."

3. who māde the red hat? _sal_

4. now can pat go to the moon? _yes_

---

1. māke the word under under the box.

2. māke the word ōver under the circle.

3. cross out the box.

under   over

1. the girl told her mother that she went __to sleep__.
   - to sleep • up the mountain • to the store

2. the elf said, "when you are good, the __pouch__ will be __good__."

3. is it good or bad to tell a lie? __bad__
   - good • bad

4. where did she say she found the pouch?
   __on the ground__
   - because she was sleeping • on the ground
   - in a house • near a store

5. what did she take from the pouch?
   __yellow mud__
   - yellow mud • good • a hound • a pouch

| she | found an old hound. |

o † (marks above words)

1. make a box around the word she.
2. make a circle under the word an.
3. make a † over the word hound.

an elf told tim, "every time you tell a lie, your feet will get bigger."

by the end of the day, tim had told so many lies that his feet were as big as elephants. tim cried. he told the elf that he would never lie again. so the elf made his feet small again.

1. who told tim that his feet would get bigger?
   __an elf__

2. did tim tell many lies? __yes__

3. why did tim's feet get as big as elephants?
   __he told so many lies.__

4. who made his feet small again? __the elf__

---

1. make the word bad in the circle.
2. make the word bad over the circle.
3. make the word dab under the circle.

bad
(bad)
dab

29

---

1. what did the girl have on her hands? __mud__
   - gold • mud • a pouch • an elf

2. the elf said, "when you are __bad__, the __pouch__ will be __bad__ to you. but when you are __good__, the __pouch__ will be __good__ to you."

3. the girl told __two__ lies.
   - six • one • lots of • two

4. the girl told her mother
   that __an elf gave her the pouch__.
   - an elf gave her the elf
   - an elf gave her the pouch
   - a pooch gave her the pouch

5. how many gold rocks were in the pouch now?
   __a thousand__
   - a thousand • ten • none • six

6. the girl said to herself, "I will keep on
   doing __good things__."
   - lots of things • bad things
   - gold things • good things

o   m
| where | did they go?

1. make a m over the word go.
2. make a box around the word where.
3. make a circle over the word where.

---

one day a girl did something that was very good. she reached into the magic pouch and found a mouse. this mouse was gold. and when it walked, it went "ding, ding, ding." three men wanted to buy the mouse, but the girl did not sell it. she kept the gold mouse.

1. was the pouch good to the girl? __yes__
2. what was in the pouch? a __gold mouse__
3. could the mouse walk? __yes__
4. who kept the gold mouse? __the girl__

---

1. make the word over under the circle.
2. make the word over over the box.
3. make a r in the circle.

over
(r)
over
[ ]

1. an elephant wanted to sit in the __sun__ .
     • sit   • lake   • sun   • walk

2. who was sitting in the elephant's spot? a __fly__
     • fun   • fan   • fat   • fly

3. the fly said, "I'll __fix you__ ."
     • fix food   • go home
     • fix you   • go to sleep

4. what did the elephant do?
   __went to sleep__
     • went to the show   • went to sleep
     • went out   • left

5. what did she see when she woke up?
   __many bugs__
     • one fly   • many men
     • lots of boys   • many bugs

6. who took the elephant away? __the bugs__
     • the fly   • a girl   • the bugs   • a hound

7. they dropped her in the __lake__ .

30

[⬚ does] ⁰ he want these trees?
         ꜱ

1. make a circle over the word he.

2. make a box around the word does.

3. make s under the word these.

---

     bill liked to jump. he would jump on the table. he would jump over the ball.
     one day he jumped on the dog. the dog barked at him so loud that bill ran and hid. so bill stopped jumping.

1. who liked to jump? __bill__

2. who barked at bill? __the dog__

3. why did he stop jumping?
   __the dog barked at him.__
     • the dog barked at him.   • the dog kissed him.
     • the dog hid him.

---

1. make a 4 in the circle.

2. make a 3 next to the 4.

3. make the word in under the 3.

---

1. a girl had a pet __goat__ .
     • goat   • coat   • boat   • gate

2. the goat ate cans, and he ate __canes__ .

3. the goat ate pans, and he ate __panes__ .

4. the goat ate capes, and he ate __caps__ .

5. who saw the big red car near the house?
the __robber__
     • goat   • farmer   • robber   • robe

[(if) you shout, you must leave.]
                   ⁹
           ⬚

1. make a g over the word leave.

2. make a circle around the word if.

3. make a box under the word shout.

---

     five elephants met on a road. one elephant said, "let's get rid of the bugs around here."
     "yes," the other elephants said.
     a bug said, "if you try to get rid of us, we will send our best man after you. and our best man is a mouse."
     the elephants ran so fast that they made a road over the hill.

1. how many elephants met on the road? __five__

2. the elephants wanted to get rid of the __bugs__ .

3. who was the bug's best man? a __mouse__

---

1. make the word in under the box.

2. make the word over in the box.

3. make the word under over the box.

         __under__
       [over]
         in

1. why was the girl's dad mad at the goat?

the goat __ate things_____.
   - hit things   - found things   - ate things

2. what did the girl's dad have?

a __red car_____
   - red goat   - red car   - red car   - white car

3. where were the girl and the goat?

in the __back yard_____

4. why did the car robber go flying? the goat __hit him__.
   - called   - hit him   - ate him   - bit him

5. the girl's dad said, "that goat

can __stay_____ with us."
   - fun   - stay   - play   - sway

6. the robber said, "I am __sore_____."

```
┌─────────────────────────────────┐
│  ~~when~~ did you stop shouting? │
│           f                      │
└─────────────────────────────────┘
```

1. make a box around the question mark.
2. cross out the word <u>when</u>.
3. make a <u>f</u> under the word <u>stop</u>.

---

look at the picture on page 158 of your reader.

1. does the girl look happy or sad? __happy___

there was a flying goat. the goat kept flying
into things. the goat said, "I can fly, but I
can't see very well."
   a mouse said, "I can't fly, but I can see. let
me sit on your back and tell you where to go."
   now the flying goat does not fly into things.

1. who said, "I can fly, but I can't see"?

__the goat___

2. who said, "I can't fly, but I can't see"?

__the mouse___

3. why did the goat fly into things?

__he could not see very well.__

4. does the goat fly into things now? __no___

5. who tells the goat where to fly? __the mouse__

31

---

1. a girl named Jane wanted to fly, __fly__, __fly__.

2. what did she want to make? a __kite___
   - fly   - kite   - bird   - tree

3. they made the kite out of __paper and_____

__string and wood_____.
   - paper and wool   - paper and birds
   - paper and string and wood

4. Jane was all set to go, __go__, __go__.

5. but her father said, "__no__, __no__, __no__."

```
┌─────────────────────────────────┐
│  does she have ~~our~~ coats?    │
│               v                  │
└─────────────────────────────────┘
```

1. make a circle around the question mark.
2. make a <u>v</u> under the word <u>does</u>.
3. cross out the word <u>our</u>.

---

look at the picture on page 160 of your reader.

1. is Jane's kite big or small? __big_____

2. is her father standing or sitting? __standing_____

a lady had a little car that would not go.
it would not go because it was in the mud.
   an elephant came to the lady and said, "if
you will give me some nuts, I will help get your
car out." so the lady gave the elephant some nuts,
and the elephant got the car out of the mud.

1. who had a little car? __a lady_____
   - an elephant   - a lady   - a man

2. why didn't the little car go?

__it was in the mud.__

3. did the elephant help the lady? __yes___

4. what did the lady give the elephant? some __nuts__

1. who wanted to fly? __Jane__
   - jan   - her dad   - jane   - pane

2. where did jane go when she held on to the kite?

   into the __sky__
   - sky   - water   - house   - barn

3. when she was over the town, she said, "I want

   to go __down__, __down__, __down__."

4. how far from town did the kite land? five __miles__
   - days   - years   - miles   - feet

5. did jane ever try flying again? __no__

☒ you want to ⬚go⬚ with us☒

1. cross out the word do.

2. make a box around the question mark.

3. make a box around the word go.

32

look at the picture on page 163 of your reader.

1. is jane holding a kite or a cloud?

   __a kite__

2. does she look happy or sad? __sad__

3. is she looking up or down? __down__

---

a kite said, "I think I will fly up in the sky."
so the kite went up and up.

five clouds said, "what are you doing up here,
kite? can't you see that we are having a meeting?"

the kite said, "I can stay here if I want."

the clouds said, "and we can make rain if
we want."

so the clouds made so much rain that the kite
went back to the ground.

1. who said, "I think I will fly up in the sky"?

   __a kite__

2. who said, "what are you doing up here?"

   __five clouds__

3. what did the clouds make to get rid of the kite?

   __rain__

---

1. the little cloud lived in the __sky__.
   - sky   - park   - barn   - sea

2. he lived with his __father and mother__.
   - mother and brother   - father and brother
   - father and mother

3. who was the best rain
   maker in the sky? the __father cloud__
   - father cloud   - mother cloud
   - brother cloud   - little cloud

4. why did the little
   cloud feel sad? __he couldn't make rain.__
   - he couldn't sleep.   - he couldn't make rain.
   - he couldn't swim.

5. why did the little cloud go far from his mother and

   father? __a wind began to blow.__
   - he was sad.   - his father made loud sounds.
   - there was no rain.   - a wind began to blow.

---

we d̶o̶n̶'t̶ have a very big ⬭car.⬭
         ^y

1. cross out the word don't.

2. make a circle around the word car.

3. make a y over the word we.

look at the picture on page 166 of your reader.

1. what are the mother cloud and the father cloud

   making? __rain__

2. does the little cloud look happy or sad? __sad__

3. which cloud is darker, the little cloud or the father

   cloud? __the father cloud__

---

a rock was in love with a tree. but the tree
was tall and the rock was small. then one day, the
wind began to blow very hard. the wind bent the
tree down to the ground. when it came near the
rock, the rock gave the tree a kiss.

1. who was in love with a tree? __a rock__

2. what bent the tree down to the ground? __the wind__

3. what did the rock give to the tree? __a kiss__

4. who was tall, the tree or the rock? __the tree__

1. why was the small cloud far from his mother and father?

__a wind was blowing.__
- a wind was blowing.   • he called for help.
- he was sad.

2. how many tears came out when he tried to cry? __none__
- lots   • none   • one   • some

3. the small deer and the mother deer were __trapped__.
- tripped   • happy   • trapped   • running

4. the little cloud wanted his mom and dad

to __make rain on the forest__.
- go away   • make rain on the forest
- get bigger

5. could they hear the little cloud? __no__

6. why not? __they were far away.__
- they were far away.   • they were too big.
- they didn't eat.

nell sat on a log.

1. make a box around the word log.

2. make a line under the word on.

3. circle the word that tells who sat on the log.

---

look at the picture on page 169 of your reader.

1. is the little cloud in the picture? __yes__

2. how many deer are in the picture? __two__

3. do you think the deer feel hot or cold? __hot__

---

tim wanted to go for a swim. but the sky was dark with clouds. tim was sad. an old man said, "don't feel sad about the clouds in the sky. they will bring rain." so tim ran in the rain and had a good time.

1. who wanted to go for a swim? __tim__

2. what was in the sky? __clouds__

3. who was sad? __tim__

4. who said, "don't feel sad about the clouds"?

__an old man__

---

1. who was the only one who could help?

the __little cloud__
- deer   • father cloud
- little cloud   • mother cloud

2. when the cloud began to shake,

he became __bigger and darker__.
- bigger and darker   • smaller and shorter
- smaller and darker

3. what started to fall from the cloud? __rain__
- snow   • rocks   • rain   • sand

4. what did the deer say? "__thank you__."
- stop that   • we're wet   • go away   • thank you

5. the mother cloud was very __proud__.
- loud   • proud   • pound   • little

don ate three cans of beans.

1. circle the word that tells who ate the beans.

2. make a line over the word three.

3. make a box under the word beans.

---

look at the picture on page 172 of your reader.

1. how many clouds are in the picture? __three__

2. who is making rain? __the little cloud__

3. do the clouds look happy or sad? __happy__

---

a mean man had a plane. he loved to fly into the clouds. the clouds said, "stop that," but the man did not stop.

then one day the man began to fly his plane into a big dark cloud. the cloud said, "booooooom." the man was afraid. now he does not fly into clouds.

1. the man loved to fly into __the clouds__.

2. who said, "stop that"? __the clouds__

3. who said, "booooooom"? __the cloud__

4. why did the man get afraid? __the cloud said,__
"__booooooom.__"
- the plane was red.   • the cloud said, "go home."
- the cloud said, "booooooom."

5. does the man fly into clouds now? __no__

1. where did the tall man and his dog go?

to the __lake__
   - shop - street - lake - store

2. the dog said, "I hate to walk, __walk__, __walk__,
but I love to __talk__, __talk__, __talk__."

3. did the dog like to swim? __no__

4. the dog said, "I love to eat things that are good,
__good__, __good__. but I hate to go hunting
for __wood__, __wood__, __wood__."

5. what did the dog do when the tall man jumped in the lake?
__she ate beans and meat.__
   - she ate the fish. - she ate beans and meat.
   - she went to sleep.

| jane (was) rIding a big fat hŏrse. |

1. make a box around the word that tells who was rIding
the hŏrse.

2. circle the word _was_.

3. make a line over the word _hŏrse_.

34

look at the picture on page 175 of your reader.

1. who is jumping in the lake? __the tall man__

2. does the tall man look happy or afraid? __afraid__

3. does the dog look happy or afraid? __happy__

---

carla saw a fire in the woods. then the wind
began to blow and the fire got bigger and
bigger. carla trIed to put out the fire, but the
fire got bigger. "help," she yelled.
and the little cloud said, "I will help."
the cloud made rain. now the fire is out.

1. who saw a fire in the woods? __carla__

2. why did the fire get bigger and bigger?
__the wind began to blow.__

3. who helped carla? __the little cloud__

4. what did the cloud make? __rain__

---

1. sandy was good at __counting__.
   - sitting - sleeping - counting - running

2. on her way to school one day she counted
__train cars__.
   - train cars - trucks - tv sets - airplanes

3. how many cars were in the train before school?
__100__
   - 2 - 50 - 20 - 100

4. how many cars were red? __50__

5. how many cars were yellow? __50__

6. what did the man say was missing? __tv sets__
   - trucks - tv sets - hams - windows

| sam kissed (jill.) |

1. circle the word that tells who sam kissed.

2. make a line under the word _kissed_.

3. make a box around the word that tells who kissed jill.

look at the picture on page 178 of your reader.

1. is sandy standing or sitting? __standing__

2. what is she looking at? __train cars__

3. is she counting the cars? __yes__

---

a girl had a hound that could count. the girl
held up three rocks and asked, "how many rocks
are here?" the dog barked three times.
the girl held up five rocks and asked, "how
many rocks are here?" the dog barked five times.

1. what could the girl's hound do? __count__

2. how many times did he bark
when she held up three rocks? __three__

3. how many times did he bark
when she held up five rocks? __five__

4. how many times would he bark
if she held up one rock? __one__

| **Accept words or numerals.** |

1. what did sandy like to do? ___count___
   • pound • hound • count • sound

2. how many cars were in
   the train before school? ___one hundred___

3. how many cars were yellow? ___fifty___

4. how many cars were red? ___fifty___

5. how many cars were in
   the train after school? ___ninety-nine___
   • one hundred • ninety-nine • two • one

6. what did the man say was missing? ___tv sets___
   • an elephant • tv sets • brooms • three cows

_____

bob met <u>jan</u> on the r̄oad.

1. make a line under the word that tells who bob met.

2. make a circle over the word bob.

3. make a box over the word r̄oad.

---

look at the picture on page 181 of your reader.

1. how many red train cars do you see? ___one___

2. what is sandy holding? ___a book___

3. how many men are standing in front of the train? ___two___

_____

bill was a mouse. bill liked to ride. he didn't
like to ride in cars. he didn't like to ride on
bikes. he loved to ride in train cars. and the
kind of train car he liked best was a box car
filled with food. he would ride and eat, ride
and eat.

1. what was bill? ___a mouse___

2. where did bill love to ride? ___in train cars___

3. what did he do when he rode
   in cars filled with food? ___eat___

4. what kind of train car did he like best? ___a box
   car filled with food___

35

---

1. how many cars were in the train when sandy went to
   school? ___one hundred___

2. how many cars were in
   the train after school? ___ninety-nine___

3. which car was missing? a ___red car___
   • white car • yellow car • black car • red car

4. sandy walked next to the rail road track until she
   reached a ___shed___.
   • shad • shed • ship • school

5. what was inside the shed?
   a ___red train car___
   • red train car • yellow train car
   • black train car

6. what was inside the train car? ___tv sets___
   • an elephant • tv sets • men • a door

_____

(jill) met [mike] at the <u>lake</u>.

1. circle the word that tells who met mike.

2. make a box around the word that tells who jill met
   at the lake.

3. make a line over the word lake.

---

look at the picture on page 184 of your reader.

1. what is inside the shed? ___a train car___

2. who is looking in the shed? ___sandy___

_____

one day sandy was in the store. a man picked
up some cans of beans. sandy counted the cans.
he had nine cans of beans. he went to pay a lady
for the cans of beans. the lady said that he had
ten cans of beans, but sandy told her that he had nine
cans of beans. sandy and the man were happy.

1. who picked up the cans of beans? ___a man___

2. who counted them? ___sandy___

3. who said that he had ten cans of beans? ___a lady___

4. who said that he had nine cans of beans? ___sandy___

1. what did sandy like to do? __count__

2. what was inside the shed?

   __a red train car__
   - dogs - a truck - a red train car
   - a yellow train car

3. what was in the train car? __tv sets__
   - tv sets - dogs - trucks - boys

4. who was hiding inside the train car? __sandy__
   - a man - sandy - many men - a truck

5. the men were going to load the tv sets into a __truck__ .
   - red train car - yellow train car - truck - boat

6. who stopped sandy? __a big man__
   - an old man - a big man - a dog - a girl

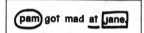

1. circle the word that tells who got mad at jane.

2. make a line under the word **at**.

3. make a box around the word that tells who pam got mad at.

36

1. what did sandy like to do? __count__

2. where was the train car? in a __shed__
   - street - shed - shad - school

3. what was inside the train car? __tv sets__
   - tv sets - an elf - a hound - three men

4. who stopped sandy when she tried to leave the shed? a __big man__
   - big dog - big cat - little man - big man

5. sandy told the man that she was looking for her __hound dog__ .
   - hound dog - socks - brother - elf

6. did the big man let her go? __yes__

7. where did she go when she left the shed? __to the train__
   - home - to the train - to the school
   - to a store

---

sid gave the ball to jan.

1. circle the word that tells who gave the ball to jan.

2. make a box around the word **to**.

3. make a line under the word that tells who sid gave the ball to.

look at the picture on page 187 of your reader.

1. what is inside the train car? __tv sets__

2. who is inside the train car? __sandy__

3. do the men see sandy? __no__

---

there once was a mean man who had a tv set. one day he kicked the set because it did not work well. then he took it out. a little girl picked it up and cleaned it up. she took it home and gave it a big hug. the tv was so happy that it worked well from that day on.

1. who kicked the tv set? __a mean man__

2. who was mean? __a man__

3. why did he kick the tv set? __it did not work well.__

4. who cleaned up the tv set? __a little girl__

5. did the tv set work well for the girl? __yes__

look at the picture on page 190 of your reader.

1. who has a hat? __the man__

2. who is holding a book? __sandy__

3. who looks mean? __the man__

---

homer was a hound who lived near the rail road yard. he had a loud bark. the man at the yard got mad at him because homer was loud. but one day the horn fell off the big train. one man said, "I will get a horn." he came back with homer. now the train has a horn, and homer can bark all he wants.

1. who had a loud bark? __homer__

2. why did the man get mad at homer?

   __because homer was loud__

3. what fell off the big train? __the horn__

4. is homer happy now? __yes__

1. sandy ran from the __shed__ .
   ● shad   ● big dog   ● shed   ● street

2. she told the cop about the missing __train car__ .
   ● truck   ● boat   ● man   ● train car

3. who counted the cars of every train? __big bill__
   ● the cop   ● big bill   ● a teacher   ● a boy

4. big bill was the man sandy had seen at the __shed__ .

5. how many cars did big bill
   say were in the train? __ninety-nine__
   ● ninety-nine   ● one hundred   ● one   ● two

6. was big bill telling a lie? __yes__

1. circle the word three.

2. make a box around the word that tells who ted kissed.

3. circle the word that tells who kissed pam.

---

look at the picture on page 193 of your reader.

1. what did sandy drop? __a book__

2. is big bill walking? __yes__

3. how many cops do you see? __one__

---

ann had a white truck. she had a bed and a
bath tub inside the truck. ann worked hard all day.
then she went home. but she didn't go home to a
house. she went home to her white truck. she
would take a bath and then go to bed.

1. who had a white truck? __ann__

2. inside the truck she had a bed and a __bath tub__ .

3. what was ann's home? __a white truck__

4. what would ann do after she took a bath?
   __go to bed__

---

1. who counted the cars on every train? __sandy__
   ● the cop   ● a teacher   ● sandy

2. big bill looked very __mean__ .
   ● neat   ● meal   ● mean   ● meat

3. where did the cop take sandy and the others?
   to the __shed__
   ● shad   ● store   ● shed   ● town

4. what did they see outside the shed?
   a __white truck__
   ● white trunk   ● white truck
   ● red truck   ● train car

5. what were the men loading into the truck?
   __tv sets__
   ● tv sets   ● train cars   ● tracks   ● trunks

6. was big bill happy? __no__

(jan) sold her bike to pam. ☐

1. circle the word that tells who sold the bike.

2. make a line under the word that tells who jan sold the
   bike to.

3. make a box under the word to.

---

look at the picture on page 196 of your reader.

1. who has her arm out? __sandy__

2. what is the man in the shed holding? __a tv set__

3. is the back of the truck open? __yes__

---

jane worked at a pet shop. one day a man
came to the pet shop with a big truck. the man
said, "jane, load this truck with pets."
   jane said, "I can load that truck with pets
very fast."
   the man did not think that she could load it
very fast. but jane did it. she loaded the truck
with one pet elephant.

1. who worked at the pet shop? __jane__

2. a man came to the pet shop with a big __truck__ .

3. what did the man want in the truck? __pets__

4. did jane load the truck very fast? __yes__

1. who went into the shed? __the cop__
   • big bill • sandy • the woman • the cop

2. who tried to leave just then? __big bill__
   • big bill • sandy • a rail road man • the cop

3. did the man tell bill to leave? __no__

4. did the cop get all the crooks inside the shed? __yes__

5. what gift did the rail road give sandy?
   a __tv set__
   • red train car • tv set • crook • truck

(Jane) had a lot of fun (at the farm.) [v over "had"]

1. circle the word that tells who had a lot of fun.

2. circle the words that tell where jane had fun.

3. make a v over the word had.

---

look at the picture on page 199 of your reader.

1. how many crooks do you see? __two__

2. how many cops do you see? __one__

3. how many tv sets do you see? __one__

| Also accept numerals. |

jean was a crook, but she was not a very good crook. one day she tried to steal a pot, but the pot was too hot to steal. she tried to steal a house, but the house was too big. she tried to steal a bug, but the bug was so small that she could not find it. jean said, "I will stop stealing."

1. what was jean? __a crook__

2. why didn't she steal the pot?
   __it was too hot.__

3. she didn't steal the house because it was too __big__.

4. why didn't she steal the bug?
   __it was so small that she could not find it.__

38

---

1. who made a toy car from a car kit? __sam__

2. who said, "you are good at reading and at making things"? his __mom__

3. what kit did sam get after he made a car? a __kite kit__
   • car kit • cat kit • kite kit • log kit

4. what was missing from the kit? a __paper__
   • paper • kite part • car part • kit

5. where did sam go to get a paper?
   __to the store__
   • to the lake • to the store
   • because he needed it • told him

6. did the man at the store have another paper? __no__

(tim) went to the park.

1. circle the word that tells who went to the park.

2. make a line over the words that tell where tim went.

3. make a line over the circle.

---

look at the picture on page 203 of your reader.

1. is sam reading a paper? __no__

2. do you see sam's toy car? __yes__

---

bob got a kit for making a toy duck. the kit had a lot of parts. bob worked hard. at last, he said, "that duck looks real." the duck ate a hole in the wall. then he ate some grass. the duck went to the pond and swam away.

1. who got a kit for making a toy duck? __bob__

2. the duck ate a hole in the __wall__.

3. then he ate some __grass__.

4. where did he go for a swim? __to the pond__

1. did sam make a kite from the parts in the kit? __yes__

2. did sam read a paper that tells how to make a kite? __no__

3. how did the kite look? __funny__
    ● green   ● on the paper   ● funny   ● good

4. who said, "I don't think it will fly"? __his mom__

5. who said, "I think it will fly"? __sam__

6. where did sam
    go with the kite? __to the park__
        ● to the lake   ● at the store
        ● because he needed it   ● to the park

7. who said, "I don't think your kite will go three feet
    from the ground"? __his mom__

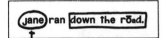

1. make a box around the 3 words that tell where she ran.

2. circle the word that tells who ran down the road.

3. make a t under the circle.

look at the picture on page 206 of your reader.

1. who is standing next to sam? __his mom__

2. how many kites do you see in the sky? __two__

3. how many girls are looking at the tent kite? __two__

Also accept numeral 2.

tom got all mixed up. one day he was holding
his hat in one hand. he was holding a hot dog in
the other. he wanted to eat the hot dog and put
the hat on his head. but he put the hot dog on
his head. then he began to eat his hat.

1. who got mixed up? __tom__

2. he was holding a hat and a __hot dog__.

3. where did he put the hot dog? __on his head__

4. what did he do with his hat? __ate it__

---

1. did sam's kite look like a dent or a tent? a __tent__

2. did sam's kite fly? __yes__

3. did it pass up the other kites? __yes__

4. who said, "I will make a paper
    that tells how to make a tent kite"? __sam__

5. who wanted to make tent kites?
    other __boys and girls__
        ● kites ● boys and girls ● moms ● streets

6. who helped sam make his paper? __his mom__

7. who said, "let's make a lot of these papers"? __sam__

8. which kites fly better
    than any other kite? __tent kites__
        ● paper kites ● small kites
        ● no kites ● tent kites

---

sid ran down the road.

1. make a box around the 3 words that tell where he ran.

2. circle the word that tells who ran down the road.

3. make a t under the circle.

look at the picture on page 209 of your reader.

1. what is sam holding? __a paper__

2. how many tent kites are flying? __two__

3. how many children are sitting on the ground? __two__

Also accept numeral 2.

one day all of the kites were flying. when
they saw the tent kite, one kite said, "look at that
funny kite. it has no tail."
    another kite said, "it looks like a flying lump.
ho, ho, ho."
    but then the kites stopped making fun of the
tent kite. the tent kite could fly better than any
other kite.

1. one day all of the __kites__ were flying.

2. who said that the tent kite looked like a flying lump?
    __another kite__

3. which kite could fly better than the other kites?
    __the tent kite__

1. what did tim have? __a hat__

2. did tim like his hat or hate his hat? __hate__ his hat

3. tim got to school on __time__ .

4. where did tim hide his hat? in __a tree__
   • a cup • the house • a tree • the snow

5. what did he see falling from the sky? __snow__
   • rain • snow • drops • birds

6. did tim hate his hat after that day? __no__

| a deer | ran to the top of the hill. |

(box around "a deer"; circle around "to the top of the hill."; v over "ran")

1. make a box around the 2 words that tell what ran to the top of the hill.

2. circle the 6 words that tell where the deer ran.

3. make a v over the word ran.

40

look at the picture on page 212 of your reader.

1. what is tim holding? __a hat__

2. is tim hot or cold? __cold__

3. is it snowing? __yes__

---

one day peg started to make a hat. she was having a lot of fun. the hat got bigger and bigger and bigger. soon the hat was too big for a boy. it was too big for a man. it was even too big for a horse. who do you think got that hat? an elephant. he liked it a lot.

1. who made the hat? __peg__

2. why couldn't a boy have the hat?
   the hat was too __big__ .

3. why couldn't a horse have the hat?
   the hat was too __big__ .

4. who got the hat? __an elephant__

---

1. who said, "my mouth is on fire"? a __fox__
   • girl • dog • fox • man

2. was his mouth on fire? __no__

3. he was trying to con her out of a c __one__ .

4. did she cool his mouth with a cone? __no__

5. what did she cool his mouth with? __water__
   • water • stones • cones

6. who ate all the ice cream? __the girl__

7. did the fox take the cone? __no__

| five men sat on the top of a mountain. |

(circle around "five men"; r under "sat")

1. circle the 2 words that tell who sat on the mountain.

2. make a line under the 6 words that tell where the men sat.

3. make a r under the word sat.

look at the picture on page 215 of your reader.

1. what is the fox sitting on? __a log__

2. does the fox look happy? __yes__

3. is ice cream going into the fox's mouth? __no__

---

an elephant and a bug met. the elephant said, "I am bigger than you. so I can do things better than you."

the bug said, "I know one thing you can't do better than me."

the elephant got mad. then he said, "what can you do better than me?"

"I can hide better than you," the bug said.

1. who did the elephant meet? __a bug__

2. who said, "I can do things better than you do"? __the elephant__

3. what could the bug do better than the elephant? __hide__

1. could the fox con the girl out of her cone? __no__

2. who went up to the ice cream stand and said, "hand me a cone"? __the fox__

3. the man at the stand said, "that will be one __dime__."
dim   dime   time

4. the fox said, "I gave you a __dime__."
cane   can   dime

5. who came up to the stand when the man was going to hand a cone to the fox? __a girl__
a man   a girl   a boy

6. did the fox ever try to con the man at the ice cream stand again? __no__

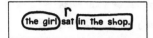

1. circle the 2 words that tell who sat in the shop.

2. make a r over the word sat.

3. make a box around the 3 words that tell where the girl sat.

a fox trIed to con a little girl. she was eating corn. he said, "close your eyes and open your mouth. I will show you a trick."

when she closed her eyes, he took her corn and began to run away. he was not looking where he was going. he ran into a tree.

the girl opened her eyes and smiled. she said, "that is a good trick."

1. who trIed to con the little girl? __a fox__

2. what was the girl eating? __corn__

3. what did the fox take from the girl? __her corn__

4. did the fox get away with the corn? __no__

5. why did the fox run into the tree?
he was not __looking where he was going__.

---

look at the picture on page 218 of your reader.

1. what is the man holding? __an ice cream cone__

2. who is walking near the ice cream stand? __a girl__

41

1. where did don work? in a __hat store__
moping   mopping   foot shop   hat store

2. why was don sad? because he was not __big__.
big   rich   fat   old

3. did don like his job or hate his job? __hate__ his job

4. what did don wish he was? a __super man__
super bug   super boy   super man   super bee

5. sometimes don would sit and __mope__.
mope   mop   run   fall

6. what did don hear? somebody __calling him__
singing   calling him   flying

7. so don opened the door and went __down the stairs__.
up the stairs   out the door   down the stairs

---

pam sent ten trees to the farm.

1. make a line over the word that tells who sent the trees.

2. make a y under the word trees.

3. circle the words that tell where the trees went.

mike was a mop. but mike was not happy. every day, a man would grab mike and dip mike into some water. then the man would take mike around the floor. then the man would let mike stand by the wall. mike said, "it is no fun to stand by the wall when you are wet and cold."

1. what was mike? __a mop__

2. who grabbed mike every day? __a man__

3. where did the man put mike when he was wet and cold?
__by the wall__

4. did mike like to stand by the wall? __no__

---

look at the picture on page 221 of your reader.

1. how many hats do you see? __three__ (or 3)

2. what is don holding? __a mop__

3. is it dark down the stairs? __yes__

1. where did don work? in a __hat store__

    hate store   barn   hat store   hand store

2. why did don mope? because he was __not a super man__

    a super man   not a super man   not little

3. the woman in the dark had a __cape and a cap__.

    cape and a cap   can and a cane   cape and a cane

4. did the woman hand something to don? __yes__

5. the woman told don to __tap__ the dime three times.

    tape   slap   tan   tap

6. did don do that? __yes__

five dogs jumped on the table.

1. make a line under the words that tell where the dogs jumped.

2. make an e over the word jumped.

3. circle the words that tell who jumped on the table.

42

there once was a super bug. that bug had a cape. that bug could fly faster than the other bugs. and that bug could bite hard. one day, a dog was going to bite a little bug. the super bug bit the dog so hard that the dog yelled and ran away.

the little bug said, "thank you, super bug." the little bug gave the super bug a kiss.

1. who could fly faster than the other bugs? __super bug__

2. who was going to bite a little bug? __a dog__

3. why did the dog run away? the super bug __bit the dog__.

4. who saved the little bug? __super bug__

5. who gave the super bug a kiss? __the little bug__

---

look at the picture on page 224 of your reader.

1. what is that woman giving don? __a dime__

2. who is bigger, the woman or don? __the woman__

3. the woman has a cape and a __cap__.

1. the woman who gave don the dime had a cap and a __cape__.

2. the woman told don to do __good things__.

    bad things   good things   funny things

3. she told don to tap the dime __three__ times.

    one   two   three   five

4. when don tapped the dime, there was the sound of __thunder__.

    thunder   cars   trains   a girl

5. did don get to be a super man? __yes__

6. where did don tape the dime? to his __arm__

    leg   arm   nose   foot

7. don had a __cape and a cap__.

    cape and a cane   cop and a hut   cape and a cap

8. was don doing good things? __no__

---

the con ran to pam's cone shop.

1. make a d over the word cone.

2. make a box around the words that tell who ran to pam's cone shop.

3. make a line under the words that tell where the con ran.

one day the super bug met a sad horse fly. the horse fly said, "I am sad because there are not any horses for me to bite. I am not a man fly. I am not a dog fly. I am not a house fly."

the super bug picked up the horse fly and took him to a horse farm. now the horse fly is happy. he can bite all the horses he wants.

1. who did the super bug meet? __a sad horse fly__

2. why was the horse fly sad? because there were no __horses__ to bite

3. where did the super bug take the horse fly? __to a horse farm__

4. is the horse fly happy on the farm? __yes__

---

look at the picture on page 3 of your reader.

1. how many holes are in the wall? __two (or 2)__

2. what is don holding? __a mop__

1. who gave don the dime?

a woman in _a cape and cap_

    a cape and cap   a house   the street

2. what did she tell don to do? _good things_

    bad things   many things   good things   nothing

3. did don do good things? _no_

4. did he open the door to the store? _no_

5. did the boys like him? _no_

6. what did he do to the car? _gave it a heave_

    fixed it   gave it a heave   sat in it   ate it

7. was don having fun? _yes_

1. circle the word that tells who felt sad.

2. make a p under the circle.

3. make a line under the word that tells how jill felt.

---

one day the super bug met a sad grass hopper. the grass hopper said, "I can't hop. my hopper does not work."

    the super bug said, "I can fix that."

    the grass hopper said, "I hope you can make me hop."

    then the super bug began to bite the grass hopper. the grass hopper said, "I'm getting out of here." and the grass hopper hopped like mad. "I can hop," he said.

1. who did the super bug meet? _a sad grass hopper_

2. why was the grass hopper sad?

because his _hopper_ did not work

3. who said, "I hope you can make me hop"? _the grass hopper_

4. what did the super bug do to make the grass hopper hop?

the super bug began to _bite the grass hopper._

---

look at the picture on page 6 of your reader.

1. what is don lifting? _a car_

2. does don look happy or sad? _happy_

3. do the boys look happy or sad? _sad_

43

---

1. don was not doing _good_ things.

2. don said, "When I worked in the store, I would mope and _mop_ ."

3. The man didn't think that don looked like a _super man_ .

4. don gave the bus a _heave_ .

    sock   heave   kiss   cow

5. Could don run fast? _no_

6. did the boys and girls like don or hate him? _hate_ him

7. Was don happy or sad? _sad_

8. did don start to mop or mope? _mope_

Pam slid fast.

1. make a box around the word that tells who slid.

2. Circle the word that tells how Pam slid.

3. make a t under the word slid.

Spot wanted to buy a bone. The man in the store said, "give me a dime for this bone."

Spot said, "I don't know what time it is." The man said, "not the time. I said, 'give me a dime.'"

Spot said, "I can't hear you. Take this dime and give me that bone."

1. What did Spot want? _to buy a bone_

2. Where did Spot go to get a bone? _to the store_

3. did Spot hear what the man said? _no_

4. The man said, "give me a dime." but what did Spot think the man said? "give me _the time_ ."

---

look at the picture on page 9 of your reader.

1. Who is running into the school? _don_

2. do the boys and girls look happy? _no_

3. What is the tall girl holding? _a book_

1. When the boys and girls ran
   away, don sat and began to m**ope**____ .

2. When he looked down, he saw
   that he did not have a cap or a c**ape**___ .

3. Where did don go? back **to the store**_____
   to the sky   to the store   to a hat   home

4. Was it dark inside the store? **yes**

5. don sat near the m**op**___ and began to mope.

6. did don begin to clean up the mess? **yes**

7. Where did the sound come from? the **stairs**_____
   sky   trees   store   stairs

That 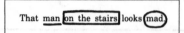 man on the stairs looks mad.

1. make a line under the word <u>man</u>.

2. make a box around the words that tell where the man is.

3. Circle the word that tells how the man looks.

44

1. Who said, "I will try to be good"? **don**____

2. did don make up for all the bad things he did? **yes**

3. did the woman give the dime back to don? **yes**

4. What stopped in front of the school? a **truck**___
   truck   trunk   tree   bus

5. Who was in the truck? a little **man**___

6. Who said, "You are too small for this job"? **don**___

7. Why did the man have the job? **his baby was sick.**
   his mother was sick.   his baby was small.
   his baby was sick.

The dog in this box sounds sad.
a

1. Circle the word that tells how the dog sounds.

2. make an <u>a</u> under the word <u>this</u>.

3. make a line over the words that tell where the dog is.

One day the super bug took off his cape. a mean
fly put on the cape. "now I am a super bug," the
fly said.

The fly tried to bite the super bug. but the
super bug said, "ho, ho. I don't need a cape to be
a super bug."

The super bug took the cape from the fly. Then
he gave the fly a super bite.

1. What did the super bug take off? **his cape**

2. Who put on the cape? **a mean fly**

3. did the super bug need the cape to be a super bug? **no**

4. What did the super bug give the fly? a super **bite**___

---

look at the picture on page 12 of your reader.

1. does don have a cape and a cap? **no**___

2. does don look sad? **yes**

3. how many tears do you see on don's cheeks? **two (or 2)**

Ten men went out hunting for bugs. each man
had a bug bag. One man filled his bag with ants.
One man filled his bag with bees. One man filled
his bag with a super bug.

The super bug jumped out of the bag. he let all
the other bugs go. Then he put the men in the bug
bags.

1. how many men went hunting? **ten**____ **(or 10)**

2. What were they hunting for? **bugs**___

3. Where did they put their bugs? **in a bug bag**

4. Who did the super bug put in the bags? **the men**

---

look at the picture on page 15 of your reader.

1. Who is bigger, don or the man? **don**

2. how many bags do you see? **three**___ **(or 3)**

3. does the man look tired? **yes**

1. Who helped the little man? **don**
2. Where did don go after he left the little man? to the **store**
3. What did the woman in the cap and cape hand don? a **dime**
4. When don tapped the dime, he saw that he had a c**ape**
   and a c**ap** | Also accept c**ap** and a c**ape**. |
5. don said, "I must do something g**ood** ."
6. did don keep the dime? **no**
7. Who has the dime now? **the little man**
8. Is the little man happy? **yes**
9. Is don happy? **yes**

| The rain feels <u>cold</u> [on] <u>her</u> nose. |

1. make a box around the word <u>her</u>.
2. make a line under the word that tells how the rain feels.
3. make a line under the words that tell where the rain is.

an elephant wanted to fly like a bird. he said,
"I will do all the things a bird does. Then I will
be able to fly like a bird."

he began to go "tweet, tweet" like a bird. Then
he made a nest like a bird. Then he tried to fly
like a bird.

but he fell on his seat. he said, "I think I will
be an elephant."

1. Who wanted to fly like a bird? **an elephant**
2. What did he say to sound like a bird? **tweet tweet**
3. What did he make? **a nest**
4. did he fly? **no**
5. What did he want to be
   after he tried to fly? **an elephant**

---

look at the picture on page 18 of your reader.

1. Is don running or flying? **flying**
2. Who is sitting in the truck? **the man**
3. don has a c**ape** and a c**ap** .
   | Also accept c**ap** and a c**ape**. |

45

1. Who had a bad leg? **the boss**
   the bum   Sid   the boss   nobody
2. Where did the boss keep her cane? in a **can**
   car   can   cane   lake
3. What did Sid try to read? **notes**
   nots   notes   pans   panes
4. One note said, "Send ten p**ine** trees."
5. did Sid do that? **no**
6. Sid made ten p**in** trees.
7. One note said, "fix the window p**ane** ."
8. but Sid made a window p**an** .
9. Was Sid doing a fine job? **no**

| The deer on the hill felt (happy.) |
| o |

1. make a line over the words that tell where the deer is.
2. Circle the word that tells how the deer felt.
3. Make an <u>o</u> under the word <u>hill</u>.

The dog hid near the bed. The old man said,
"I see you there, there, there. You can't give me a
scare, scare, scare."

The dog had a mean mask. he jumped at the
man. The man ran from the house.

The dog said, "Yes, I can, can, can scare that
man, man, man."

1. Who hid near the bed? **the dog**
2. What did the dog have? **a mean mask**
3. did the dog scare the man? **yes**
4. The dog said, "Yes, I can, can, can scare that m**an** ,
   m**an** , m**an** ."

---

look at the picture on page 21 of your reader.

1. The note says, "Send ten **pine trees** ."
2. how many pin trees do you see? **four (or 4)**
3. What is Sid holding? **a pin tree**

1. did Sid read well? __no__

2. One note said, "T**ape** _____ the oak tree near the door."

3. Is that what Sid did? __no__

4. One note said, "Send a c**one** _____ to Sam's tree farm."

5. What did Sid send to the tree farm? __a con__

6. Where did Sid call to get a con? __the jail__
   the tree farm   the man
   the jail   after he made trees

7. Who said, "I am really doing a good job"? __Sid__

8. Was Sid doing a good job? __no__

9. Sid said, "The boss will be **proud** of me."
   pouch   proud   sore   tired

```
That girl walks slowly.
  P
```

1. make a p under the word That.

2. make a line over the word that tells how the girl walks.

3. make a line under the words that tell who walks slowly.

One day Sandy counted dogs at the dog farm. On her way to school, she counted ninety dogs. When she came home from school, she counted ninety-nine dogs. She asked, "Why are there more now?"
a mother dog said, "There are more dogs because I got nine baby dogs today."

1. Who counted the dogs? __Sandy__

2. how many dogs did she count on her way to school? __ninety__

3. how many dogs did she count after school? __ninety-nine__

4. how many baby dogs did the mother dog get that day? __nine__

Also accept numerals.

look at the picture on page 24 of your reader.

1. The note says, "__Tape__ the oak tree near the door."

2. Is Sid tapping the tree? __yes__

3. Is the tree growing in the ground? __no__

46

1. Did Sid send pine trees or pin trees? __pin__ trees

2. Did Sid send a cone to the farm or a con to the farm? a __con__

3. Did Sid tap the tree or tape the tree? __tap__ the tree

4. One note said, "Plant seeds on the __slope__."
   slope   slop   slip   ground

5. Where did Sid plant the seeds? in the sl**op**

6. Who was walking with her cane? __the boss__

7. Who got very mad? __the boss__

8. Who was very sad? __Sid__

```
A car on the road sounds loud.
```

1. Make a box around the words that tell where the car is.

2. Circle the word that tells how the car sounds.

3. Make a line over the word road.

There once was a kite crook. This crook robbed stores. Then he would jump on his kite and fly away. "Ho, ho," he said. "Nobody can get me when I have my kite."
One day a cop said, "I can stop you." He grabbed a log and tossed it. The log hit the kite. The kite hit the ground. Then the crook fell to the ground. The cop said, "I've got you now."

1. The crook had a __kite__.

2. Who said, "Nobody can get me when I have my kite"? __the kite crook__

3. Who said, "I can stop you"? __a cop__

4. What did the cop toss at the kite? __a log__
   a cop   a dog   a log

Look at the picture on page 27 of your reader.

1. What is Sid planting? __seeds__

2. The note says, "Plant seeds __on the slope__."

3. What is the name of the plant shop? __Lin's Plant Shop__

1. Who dropped her cane into the can? _**the boss**_____

2. Did Sid plant seeds in
   the slop or on the slope? __**in the slop**_____

3. Did he send out pin trees or pine trees? __**pin**__ trees

4. Did Sid make a pan or a pane for the window? _**a pan**____

5. Did Sid send a cone to the
   farm or a con to the farm? __**a con**____

6. Did Sid tap the oak tree or tape that tree? ___**tap**____ the tree

7. Who was very, very sad? __**Sid**_____

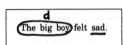

| d |
| The big boy felt <u>sad</u>. |

1. Make a <u>d</u> over the word <u>big</u>.

2. Circle the words that tell who felt sad.

3. Make a line under the word that tells how the big boy felt.

Jane liked to make big things. Once she made
a hat for her brother, Walter. That hat was so big
that it fell over his ears. It fell over his nose.
It came down to his feet.

He said, "I will fix this hat." He cut three
holes in it. One hole was for his head. Two holes
were for his arms. He said, "This hat is not a good
hat. But it is a good coat."

1. Who made the hat? __**Jane**_____

2. Who had the hat on? __**Walter**_____

3. Why didn't the hat
   sit on his head? __**It was so big.**_____

4. How many holes did he cut in the hat? _**three (or 3)**__

5. He said, "It is a good __**coat**___."

Look at the picture on page 30 of your reader.

1. Does the boss look happy or mad? __**mad**_____

2. What is on the window? __**a pan**____

3. What is the boss holding? __**a note**_____

47

---

1. Who said, "I don't read very well"? ___**Sid**_____

2. Who said, "I will teach you how to read"? _**the boss**___

3. Did Sid read well when a week went by? _**yes**__

4. One note said, "Tape a cap to my __**cape**__."

5. Did these notes fool Sid? _**no**__

6. Can Sid read the notes now? _**yes**__

7. Does Sid feel happy or sad? __**happy**___

| That cow | on the road | ran fast. |
| **e** | | |

1. Make a box around the words that tell where the cow is.

2. Make an <u>e</u> under the word <u>That</u>.

3. Make a line over the word that tells how the cow ran.

The boss had a cane can. One day, Sid took the
cane can. When the boss came back to the shop, she
was mad. "I left the cane can here," she said. "But
now it is not here. Where is it?"

Sid said, "I planted a tree in the cane can."

So now the cane can is not a cane can. It is a
tree pot.

1. Who took the cane can? __**Sid**_____

2. Who got mad? __**the boss**___

3. What did Sid plant in the cane can? _**a tree**___

4. Now the cane can is a tree __**pot**___.

Look at the picture on page 33 of your reader.

1. Do you see a pan on the window? _**no**___

2. Is Sid reading? _**yes**___

1. What was Dan? a __dog__
2. Who did Dan go to school with? __Ann__
   Sam   Ann   a man   fast
3. Who said, "Take that
   dog out of this school"? __Ann's teacher__
   Dan   Ann's mother   Ann's father   Ann's teacher
4. Who said, "But this dog is very smart"? __Ann__
5. Who began to read to himself? __Dan__
6. Who said, "I will be your teacher"? __Dan__
7. Some of the children gave Dan __a kiss__.
   a kiss   a teacher   a hug   a rug
8. They said, "We h__ope__ that Dan will be our
   teacher from now on."

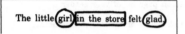

The little (girl) [in the store] felt (glad).

1. Circle the word that tells how the little girl felt.
2. Make a box around the words that tell where the little girl is.
3. Circle the word girl.

48

Once there was a man who was walking down a road.
A dog came by in her car. "Do you want a ride?" the
dog asked.
   The man said, "Where are you going?"
   "To town to sell my car," said the dog.
   "I need a car," said the man. "Sell it to me."
   "Sold," said the dog.
   Now the man is in the car and the dog is walking.

1. Where was the dog going? __to town__
2. What did the dog want to do?
   She wanted to sell __her car__.
3. Did the dog sell the car? __yes__
4. Who has the car now? __the man__

All the big dogs are sleepy.

Circle every dog that is sleepy.

---

1. Who did a fine job as a teacher? __Dan__
2. The teacher said, "I can let Dan be a teacher's __helper__"
   book   holder   helder   helper
3. How did Dan feel? __proud__
   bad   sour   proud   loud
4. How did Ann feel? __proud__
5. Do the boys and girls come to school early or late? __early__
6. They say that their teacher is very sm__art__.

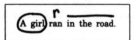

(A girl) ran in the road.
      r

1. Make an r over the word ran.
2. Make a line over the words that tell where the girl ran.
3. Circle the words that tell who ran in the road.

Once there was a girl who liked to show off. She
showed off when she ran. She showed off when she
talked. She even showed off when she ate. One day she
was running and showing off. She was running very
fast. Three other girls were looking at her. And she was
looking at the three girls. She did not see a big tree.
She ran into that tree. Now she is in bed. The only one
who sees her show off now is her dad.

1. What did the girl like to do? __show off__
2. Who was looking at the girl? __three girls__
3. Why didn't she see the big tree?
   because she was __looking at the girls__
4. What did she run into? __a tree__
5. Who does the girl show off to now? __her dad__

All the little girls are smart.

Circle every girl who is smart.

1. The tiger was __tame__ .
   lame   old   tame   time

2. Did he bite children? __no__

3. What did he like to eat? __ice cream__
   ice   ice bits   ice cream   ice skates

4. Did the tiger have any cash? __no__

5. What was in his pouch? __stones__
   stops   cones   stones   rocks

6. Did the man like the stones? __yes__

7. Who said, "What will you do with
   a big cone and some string"? __the man__

8. Who said, "Wait and see"? __the tiger__

9. The tiger made the cone into a h__at__ .

| The boy felt |cold| in the rain. |

1. Make a box around the word that tells how the boy felt.

2. Make a box around the words that tell where the boy is.

3. Make a line over the words that tell who felt cold.

One day, the boss left a note for Sid. Here
is what that note said: "Tape my cane with a bit
of white tape. The white tape is in the tape can."
   Do you think Sid did what the note said? Yes,
he did. After he looked at the note, he got the
white tape and taped the cane.

1. Who left the note for Sid? __the boss__

2. The note told Sid to __tape__ a cane.

3. Where was the white tape? __in the tape can__
   in the tap can   in the tape can

4. Sid got the tape and taped the __cane__ .

| All the big horses are tired. |

Circle every horse that is tired.

49

---

1. Did the girl ask, "How are you"? __yes__

2. Did the girl ask, "Who are you"? __no__

3. Spot said, "That girl wants to know __who I am__ ."
   where I am   how I am
   who I am   what I am

4. Who asked, "Where are you going"? __Spot__

5. Who said, "I'm going to the mall in town"? __the girl__

6. Spot said to herself, "That girl said that she will __fall__ ."
   call a cop   fall   go to the mall   sit in the hall

7. Who did Spot and the girl meet? __a pig__

8. What was that pig doing? __crying__
   crying   flying   buying   trying

| v |
| Pam tossed the red box (into the lake.) |

1. Make a line under the word that tells who tossed the red box.

2. Make a v over the word tossed.

3. Circle the words that tell where Pam tossed the red box.

Dan the dog was a teacher's helper. One day a
boy came to school. That boy did not see well. Dan
said, "I can teach you to read well. But first, you
must get glasses." So Dan took the boy to get
glasses.
   Then Dan began to teach the boy to read. The
boy said, "It is fun to read when you can see well."

1. Who was the teacher's helper? __Dan__

2. The boy did not __see__ well.
   hear   eat   see

3. Dan took the boy to get __glasses__ .
   food   glasses   books

4. Then Dan began to teach the boy to __read__ .
   spell   rest   read

| All the fat pigs are happy. |

Circle every pig that is happy.

1. The girl was t **all** _____ .

2. She was going with Spot to the m **all** _____ .

3. On their way, they met a p **ig** _____ .

4. The pig was crying because he could not find his w **ig** _____ .

5. The pig said, "I want that big ___**yellow**___ wig."

      yelling   red   black   yellow

6. Who began to cry when the girl gave the pig his wig? **Spot** _____

> That [old] car (on the hill) sounds <u>loud</u>.

1. Circle the words that tell where the old car is.

2. Make a box around the word <u>old</u>.

3. Make a line under the word that tells how the old car sounds.

50

    Once there was a hen who said, "I love to eat." So she began to eat. She ate for one day. Then she ate for another day. Then she said, "I will eat some more." So she ate some more. She got fatter and fatter.

    At last, she said, "I think I will leave this house and go for a walk." She left the house and took a walk. She walked and walked. She said, "Walking is better than getting fatter."

1. What did the hen love to do? **eat** _____

2. Why did she get so fat? because she **ate** ___ so much

3. Did the hen go out for a walk? **yes** _____

4. She said, "Walking is better than ___**getting fatter**___ ."

> Every little horse can run fast.

Circle every horse **that** can run fast.

1. The mother duck found an egg that was ___**big**___ .

    hatched   big   little   white

2. What happened when the funny-looking duckling tried to walk?

He ___**fell**___ .

    ran   fell   cried   walked

3. The other ducklings called him **names** ___ .

    names   nams   gams   nothing

4. What did the ugly duckling become? a ___**swan**___

    duck   swan   goose   caboose

5. Where did the other ducks see the swan? **on the pond**

    on the porch   under the pond
    on the pond   in the stream

6. Did they think the swan was ugly? **no** ___

7. Did the ducks get to be good friends with the swan? **yes** ___

8. What is the title of this story?

The Ugly Duckling

> (Five dogs) were <u>sad</u>.

1. Circle the words that tell who were sad.

2. Make a t over the word <u>were</u>.

3. Make a line under the word that tells how the dogs felt.

    Once there was a little dog who lived in a yard. There was a big wall around this yard. The little dog said, "I want to be with other dogs, but I do not see other dogs."

    The little dog got bigger and bigger. Soon he was so big that he said, "I think I can jump over the wall." And he did. He found lots of other dogs on the other side of the wall. Now the little dog is not sad. Now the little dog is not little.

1. What was around the little dog's yard? **a big wall** _____

2. The little dog said, "I want to be with other ___**dogs**___ ."

3. When the little dog got bigger, he **jumped** ___ the wall.

    ate   lumped   jumped

4. Now the little dog is not s **ad** ___ .

5. Now the little dog is not l **ittle** ___ .

> Every dog with spots eats grass.

Circle every dog that eats grass.

1. The kitten did not have a ___**home**___ .
   bone   snow   home   bowl

2. Was the kitten happy or sad? **sad**

3. Why didn't the kitten stay
   in the mail box? It was too ___**dark**___ .
   little   big   dark   fat

4. It started to ___**snow**___ .
   snow   rain   fog   sleet

★★★★★★★★★★★★★★★★★★★★★★★★★★★★★★★★★★★

1. Did Sid tap the oak tree or tape the oak tree?
   ___**tap**___ the oak tree (p. 22)

2. Who told Sid, "I will teach you to read"?
   ___**the boss**___ (p. 31)

3. Did Sid become good at reading? ___**yes**___ (p. 32)

┌─────────────────────────────┐
│ The ant (was) small.   │
└─────────────────────────────┘

1. Circle the word was.

2. Make a line under the words that tell who was small.

3. Make a line over the word that tells how the ant looked.

One day Spot met a boy. The boy said, "I am going to school."

Spot said, "You should not go to the pool. You should be in school."

The boy said, "I am going to school. Why do you think I have my lunch box?" The boy held up his lunch box.

Spot said, "Did you say you have lunch rocks? I don't think they would be very good to eat."

The boy said, "I have a lunch box, not lunch rocks."

1. Spot met a ___**boy**___ .

2. The boy said he was going to s___**chool**___ .

3. But Spot said, "You should not go to the ___**pool**___ ."

4. The boy said, "Why do
   you think I have my ___**lunch box**___ ?"

5. Spot did not think it would be very good to eat lunch ___**rocks**___ .

┌─────────────────────────────┐
│ Every fat cow is slow.   │
└─────────────────────────────┘

Circle every slow cow.

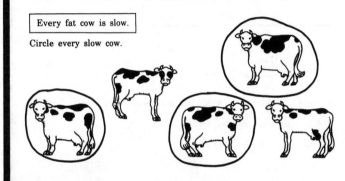

1. What is the title of this story?
   The Kitten's New Home

2. The kitten was sad because she did not have a ___**home**___ .

3. The girl asked the kitten,
   "Would you like to live on our ___**farm**___ ?"
   tree   farm   street   house

4. The girl said, "The cows give lots of ___**milk**___ ."
   mail   meat   milk   kittens

5. What didn't the girl have on her farm? a ___**kitten**___
   cow   kitten   barn   sheep

6. Who jumped into the girl's arms? ___**the kitten**___

7. Who loved that kitten? ___**the girl**___

★★★★★★★★★★★★★★★★★★★★★★★★★★★★★★★★★★★

1. What did the tame tiger like to eat? ___**ice cream**___ (p.38)

2. Did the tame tiger give the man cash or stones? **stones** (p.38)

3. The tiger made the cone into a ___**hat**___ . (p.39)

┌─────────────────────────────┐
│ The dog (was) [tired].   │
│   □   │
└─────────────────────────────┘

1. Circle the words that tell who was tired.

2. Make a box around the word that tells how the dog felt.

3. Make a box under the word was.

There was a mouse that liked to kick a ball. The mouse kicked the ball all day.

One day, the mouse was kicking the ball. A cat said, "I am going to eat this mouse." The cat opened its mouth. The mouse kicked the ball into the cat's mouth.

The mouse said, "Ha, ha. You do not have a mouse in your mouth. You have a ball in your mouth."

1. The mouse liked to kick a ___**ball**___ .

2. A cat wanted to eat the ___**mouse**___ .

3. What does the cat have in its mouth now? ___**a ball**___

4. Who said, "Ha, ha"? ___**the mouse**___

┌─────────────────────────────┐
│ Every little boy can jump rope. │
└─────────────────────────────┘

Circle the boys who can jump rope.

1. How many ghosts lived in the old house? __six__ (or **6**)

2. How many ghosts were mean? __five__ (or **5**)

3. Boo was not a __mean__ ghost.
   old   mean   big   fat

4. What did Boo like to do? __make everybody happy__
   make everybody happy   make people mad
   act mean   scare farmers

5. Were the people in town afraid of Boo? __yes__

6. Were the other ghosts he lived with afraid of Boo? __no__

7. What is the title of this story? __Boo the Ghost__

★★★★★★★★★★★★★★★★★★★★★★★★★★★★★★

1. Spot and the tall girl met a __pig__ . (p.42)

2. Spot and the tall girl were on their way to the __mall__ (p.42)

3. What did the pig want? a __wig__ (p.44)

```
            s
(Six cats) sat in a tree.
```

1. Make a line under the words that tell where the cats were.

2. Circle the words that tell who sat in the tree.

3. Make an s over the word sat.

52

One day Spot was walking down the street in her big yellow wig. A wind came up and her wig went flying into the sky. An eagle was flying near Spot. This eagle was a bald eagle. The wig landed on his head. Then the eagle said, "Now I am not a bald eagle. I am a yellow eagle."

1. Spot had on her big __yellow__ __wig__ .

2. What made the wig fly away? __the wind__
   the sun   the moon   the wind

3. Who got the wig? __an eagle__

4. Is the eagle bald now? __no__

Every big fish eats plants.

Circle every fish that eats plants.

1. What is the title of this story?
   __Boo Leaves the House__

2. Who was sitting in his seat, reading a book? __Boo__

3. Which ghost said, "We don't care where you go"?
   __the biggest ghost__
   the smallest ghost   the oldest ghost
   the biggest ghost   the fastest ghost

4. Who did Boo see crying near the stream? __a frog__

5. What did the frog say he really was? a __king__
   monster   king   queen   ghost

6. Did the frog think that Boo could help him? __no__

★★★★★★★★★★★★★★★★★★★★★★★★★★★★★★

1. A mother duck found an egg that was __big__ . (p.47)
   little   big   white

2. What did the ugly duckling become? __a swan__ (p.48)
   a duck   a man   a swan

3. Did the ducks and the swan become friends? __yes__ (p.48)

```
              v
(A fish) jumped [in the water.]
```

1. Circle the words that tell who jumped.

2. Make a box around the words that tell where the fish jumped.

3. Make a v over the word jumped.

One day the con fox said, "I need a good meal." So he went to a hot dog stand. Then he began to sing and sing. He did not sing well.
   The man said, "Get out of here."
   But the con fox did not stop. At last, the man got so mad that he began to throw hot dogs at the fox. The fox said, "Thank you. I need a good meal."

1. The fox said, "I need a good __meal__ ."

2. So he went to a __hot__ __dog__ stand.

3. Who began to sing? __the con fox__

4. Why did the man tell the fox to go away?
   The fox __did not sing well.__

5. What did the man throw at the fox? __hot dogs__

Jane has all the big kites.

Circle every kite that Jane has.

Name_____ Worksheet **105** Side **1**

1. Who said, "I will help you"? **Boo**

2. Who said, "The monster is in my castle"? **the frog**

3. Boo floated over the **town** .
   town   lake   sky   moon

4. When Boo floated near the castle, the **hounds**
   began to howl.
   ghosts   hounds   cows   monster

5. Who said, "I'll turn you into a frog or a toad"? the **monster**
   king   ghost   monster   hound

6. The monster was holding a gold **rod** .
   hat   mouse   rod   toad

7. Who said, "I must get that magic rod from the monster"? **Boo**

8. What is the title **Boo Goes to the Castle**
   of this story? _____

★★★★★★★★★★★★★★★★★★★★★★★★★★★★★★★★★★★

1. Who worked for the boss? **Sid** (p. 19)

2. Did Sid send a cone to the
   farm or a con to the farm? a **con** (p. 23)

3. Did the note tell Sid to plant
   seeds on the slope or in the slop? **on the slope** (p. 25)

┌─────────────────────────────────────┐
│   r   │
│ The snow on the hill looks white. │
└─────────────────────────────────────┘

1. Make an r over the word snow.
2. Circle the word white.
3. Make a box around the words that tell where the snow is.

Worksheet **105** Side **2**

There was an elephant that liked to jump.
Everybody tried to get him to stop jumping.
He was making a mess. One day a tiger said,
"I will stop his jumping." The tiger made a
big hole in the ground. He put grass over
the hole. Then he told the elephant to jump
on that grass. When the elephant jumped, he
fell into the hole. Fifty bugs tickled him
and tickled him. The elephant said he would
not jump again. Now everybody is happy.

1. Who liked to jump? **an elephant**

2. The tiger made a h **ole** in the ground.

3. Fifty **bugs** tickled the elephant.

┌──────────────────────────────────┐
│ Pam has all of the little kites. │
└──────────────────────────────────┘

Circle every kite that Pam has.

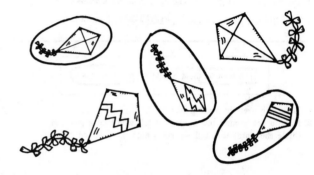

53

Name_____ Worksheet **106** Side **1**

1. Boo wanted to get the magic **rod** from the monster.

2. Who tried to scare the monster? **Boo**

3. Was the monster scared? **no**

4. Did the monster laugh? **yes**

5. What did Boo have growing from his back? a big **fin**
   fan   fun   fat   fin

6. Who was really scared? **Boo**

7. Boo was part **fish** and part ghost.
   frog   fig   fish   fear

8. Did Boo think of a plan? **yes**

★★★★★★★★★★★★★★★★★★★★★★★★★★★★★★★★★★★

1. The kitten didn't like the
   mail box because it was too **dark** . (p. 50)
   big   light   dark   wet

2. The kitten didn't like the
   fish bowl because it was too **wet** . (p. 51)
   big   light   dark   wet

3. Where did the girl take the kitten? to a **farm** (p. 53)

┌──────────────────────────────────┐
│ The rock feels hard in my hand. │
└──────────────────────────────────┘

1. Circle the words that tell what feels hard.
2. Circle the word that tells how the rock feels.
3. Make a line over the words that tell where the rock is.

Worksheet **106** Side **2**

One day a car stopped near Spot. A dog
and a cow were in that car. Spot said, "Who are
you?"
   The dog said, "Bark."
   Spot said, "So your name is Mark. Where are
you going, Mark?"
   The cow said, "Moooooo."
   Spot said, "So you are going to the zoo. I
hope you have fun."

1. What stopped near Spot? **a car**

2. Who was in that car? a **dog** and a **cow**

3. What did Spot think the dog said? **Mark**

4. What did Spot think the cow said? **zoo**

┌──────────────────────────────────────┐
│ Sandy counted all of the little balls.│
└──────────────────────────────────────┘

Circle every ball that Sandy counted.

1. What is the title of this story? __Boo's Plan Works__

2. Boo had a plan for getting the gold __rod__ from the monster.

3. Who said, "I found somebody you can't scare"? __Boo__

4. How many ghosts jumped up from the table? __five__ (or **5**)

5. Which ghost made himself as big as a horse?

   the __biggest ghost__
   gold house   biggest ghost
   oldest ghost   smallest ghost

6. What did the five ghosts do when they saw Boo's fins and tail?

   They started to __laugh__ .
   laugh   cry   think   get scared

7. Were the five ghosts afraid to go to the monster's castle? __no__

★★★★★★★★★★★★★★★★★★★★★★★★★★★★★★★★

1. Who told Sid, "I will teach you to read"? __the boss__
   (p. 31)

2. Did Sid get to be good at reading? __yes__ (p. 32)

3. Does Sid feel happy or sad? __happy__ (p. 32)

[The monster held a gold rod over the toad.]

1. Make a **b** over the word <u>held</u>.
2. Make a box around the words that tell who held a gold rod.
3. Circle the words that tell where he held the gold rod.

Every day a mean bird would scare people in town. That bird said, "It is fun to scare people. So I'll scare them at night." So the bird began to play tricks on people at night. Then one night a man shouted at the bird. The bird got scared. Now the bird does not scare people any more.

1. This story is about a mean __bird__ .

2. What did that bird like to do? __scare__ people

3. Who shouted at the bird? __a man__

[Sam made all of the little dresses.]

Circle every dress that Sam made.

54

1. What is the title of this story? __The Ghosts Meet the Monster__

2. Who began to howl when the ghosts got near the castle? the __hounds__
   mouse   house   hounds   horse

3. Did one of the ghosts scare the hounds? __yes__

4. Who was sitting at the table when the ghosts floated in? __the monster__

5. What broke into a thousand pieces? __the table__

6. Who said, "I'm leaving"? __the monster__

7. Did Boo pick up the magic rod? __no__

8. Who grabbed the magic rod? the __biggest ghost__
   old hound   monster   Boo   biggest ghost

★★★★★★★★★★★★★★★★★★★★★★★★★★★★★★★★

1. The woman told Don to do __good__ things. (p. 222- Storybook 1)

2. The woman handed Don a __dime__ . (p. 222- Storybook 1)

3. Don __taped__ the dime to his __arm__ (p. 1 - Storybook 2)

[The castle was on the hill.]

1. Make a line under the words that tell what was on the hill.
2. Circle the word <u>was</u>.
3. Make a line over the words that tell where the castle was.

One day the con fox said, "I will get some cash from a store. I will get a fish pole. I will drop a line down to the cash box and steal some cash."

So the con fox got on top of the store. He dropped his line down into the store. Then he lifted it as hard as he could. But he didn't have a cash box on the end of his line. He had a big cop on the end of his line. Now the con fox is in jail. He is a con.

1. Who said, "I will get cash from a store"? __the con fox__

2. What did he get? a __fish pole__

3. Was a fish on his line? __no__

4. What was on his line? __a big cop__

5. Where is the con fox now? __in jail__

[Every elephant is in the zoo.]

Circle every animal that is in the zoo.

1. What is the title of this story? __The Ghosts Turn on Boo__

2. Did the biggest ghost try to turn Boo into a leaf? __yes__

3. Did the biggest ghost turn Boo into a leaf? __no__

4. Who said, "This thing doesn't work"? __the biggest ghost__

5. The biggest ghost said, "Bine bin, f__ine__ f__in__."

6. Did the biggest ghost turn into a big yellow flower? __no__

7. Were the other ghosts sad when one ghost turned into a leaf? __no__

8. Were there words on the side of the rod? __yes__

9. Did the ghost read these words? __no__

10. The ghost holding the rod said, "I can't __read__."

★★★★★★★★★★★★★★★★★★★★★★★★★★★★★★★★★

1. Could Don run fast when he was a super man? __yes__ (p.8)

2. Who made a hole in the school? __Don__ (p.8)

3. Did the boys and girls like Don or hate him? __hate him__ (p.9)

___

| That red truck | ᶜ was <u>outside</u>.

1. Make a box around the words that tell what was outside.
2. Make a line under the word that tells where the red truck was.
3. Make a <u>c</u> over the word <u>was</u>.

A monster named Ib had the biggest teeth you have seen. He would show his teeth to people and they would scream. Then they would run away. One day Ib showed his teeth to a little girl. But she didn't scream and run away. She said, "Your teeth are yellow. They need a good brushing." She took out her tooth brush and brushed the monster's teeth. Now the monster is happy. He has white teeth.

1. What was the monster's name? __Ib__

2. Ib had big __teeth__.

3. Did the little girl run away? __no__

4. What did she do to the monster's teeth? __brushed them__
   hit them   sat on them   brushed them

5. Why is the monster happy now? __He has white teeth.__

___

| Linda picked every big flower. |

Circle all the flowers that Linda picked.

---

1. How many ghosts could read the words? __one__

2. Which ghost could read the words? __Boo__

3. Boo said, "Bit bite, ben __bean__."

4. Did the ghosts feel mean then? __no__

5. Did a ghost feel like helping a farmer? __yes__

6. Did Boo turn the flower into a monster or a ghost? __a ghost__

7. Who said magic words to make Boo's tail go away? __Boo__

★★★★★★★★★★★★★★★★★★★★★★★★★★★★★★★★★

1. Who worked for the boss? __Sid__ (p.19)

2. Did Sid send a cone to the farm or a con to the farm? __a con__ (p.23)

3. Did the note tell Sid to plant seeds in the slop or on the slope? __on the slope__ (p.25)

___

(A <u>green</u> frog scared the ghosts.)

1. Circle the words that tell who scared the ghosts.
2. Make a line under the word <u>ghosts</u>.
3. Make a line over the word <u>green</u>.

Once there was a very sad snake. That snake could not kick a ball. All the other animals kicked the ball. But snakes do not have legs.

Then one day the snake said, "I will use my head." And she did. Now she can make the ball go as far as the other animals can. But the snake doesn't kick the ball. She hits the ball with her head.

The other animals all say, "That snake can really use her head."

1. Why was the snake sad? She couldn't __kick a ball__

2. Snakes do not have l__egs__.

3. Who said, "I will use my head"? __the snake__

4. Can the snake make the ball go far? __yes__

___

| If a horse is running, she is old. |

Circle every horse that is old.

1. Boo had turned the mean ghosts into ___**smiling**___ ghosts.
        sitting   smiling   mean

2. Boo said, "Hog, sog, bumpy ___**log**___ ."

3. Who said, "You must come to live with me"? ___**the king**___

4. Who was shy? ___**Boo**___

5. Did Boo go to live with the king? ___**yes**___

6. People went out at night to find ___**ghosts**___ .
       monsters   farmers   ghosts

★★★★★★★★★★★★★★★★★★★★★★★★★★★★★★

1. Where were Spot and
   the tall girl going? ___**to the mall**___ (p.42)

2. Did Spot hear well? ___**no**___ (p.41)

3. What did the pig want? ___**a wig**___ (p.44)

The girl sat ⌐r⌐ (in her tent)

1. Make a box around the words that tell who sat in the tent.

2. Circle the words that tell where the girl sat.

3. Make an r over the word sat.

56

1. Who was going to genie school? ___**Ott**___

2. Could Ott do a lot of genie tricks? ___**no**___

3. Was Ott the best of those in genie school? ___**no**___

4. What did Ott make when the teacher told him to make an apple?
   ___**an alligator**___
       an alligator   an apple   a ship   a genie

5. What did Ott make when the teacher told him to make gold?
   a pot of b___**eans**___

6. Who ran into the school? ___**an old woman**___
       a child   a teacher   an old woman   a yellow bottle

7. Who would have to go to the yellow bottle?
   one of the ___**children from school**___
       old genies   teachers   children from school

★★★★★★★★★★★★★★★★★★★★★★★★★★★★★★

1. What did the monster turn the king into? ___**a frog**___ (p.58)

2. The monster had a rod made of ___**gold**___ . (p.61)

3. The monster made Boo part ___**fish**___ and part ghost. (p.64)

(Three mean ghosts) [went] to the farm.

1. Circle the words that tell who went to the farm.

2. Make a box around the word went.

3. Make a line over the words that tell where the ghosts went.

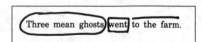

    The con fox said, "It is getting cold out.
I need a new coat. So I will go out and con
somebody out of a coat." So the con fox went
out. He saw some white coats near a farm
house. But when he tried to grab those coats,
he found out that they were ghosts. So the
con fox ran back to his cold house.

1. Who said, "It is getting cold out"? ___**the con fox**___

2. What did the con fox want? ___**a coat**___
       a coat   a box   a sheet

3. So he went to a farm ___**house**___ .

4. What were the coats? ___**ghosts**___
       men   farmers   ghosts

| If a girl is swimming, she is tall. |

Circle every girl who is tall.

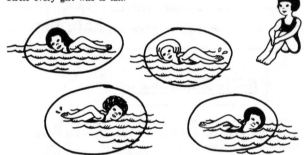

    An elephant lived with jumping bugs. That
elephant never saw another elephant. All he
saw was bugs. So the elephant tried to be a
bug. He tried to jump like a bug. But every
time he jumped he made a hole in the ground.
The bugs were getting mad at him. They kept
saying, "You are not a bug. Stop trying to jump
around."
    One day the elephant met five other
elephants. Now the elephant doesn't jump like
a jumping bug. He walks like the other
elephants.

1. Who did the elephant live with? ___**jumping bugs**___

2. What did the elephant make when he jumped?
   a ___**hole**___ in the ground

3. Who said, "Stop trying to jump around"? ___**the bugs**___

4. Does the elephant jump like a jumping bug now? ___**no**___

| If a hat is spotted, it is old. |

Circle every hat that is old.

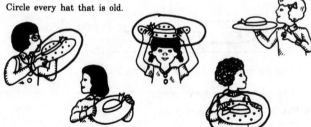

Name_____

1. What is the name of the genie in this story? __Ott__

2. Who said, "No, no. These children cannot go to work as genies"?
__the teacher__

3. Who said, "I will give the children a test"? __the old woman__

4. The old woman said, "Make a __peach__ appear on the floor."

5. Did Ott make a peach or a beach? a __beach__

6. Which genie was sent to the yellow bottle? __Ott__

7. What is the title of this story?
__Ott Takes a Test__

★★★★★★★★★★★★★★★★★★★★★★★★★★★★★★★★★

1. How many ghosts lived with Boo? __Five__ (p.54) (or **5**)

2. Could any of those ghosts read? __no__ (p.75)

3. Which ghost could read the words on the magic rod? __Boo__
(p.75)

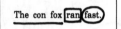

The con fox (ran) (fast.)

1. Make a box around the word ran.

2. Circle the word that tells how he ran.

3. Make a line under the words that tell who ran fast.

One day Boo was walking down the street. Boo had his magic rod. The monster jumped out and tried to take the rod from Boo. Boo held onto the rod and said, "Bid bide sap sape."

And what do you think happened to the monster? She turned into a teacher. She smiled. She was nice. She was smart. She was one of the best teachers you have ever seen.

1. What was Boo holding? the magic __rod__

2. Who wanted to take the rod from Boo? __the monster__

3. Who said magic words? __Boo__

4. What did the monster turn into? __a teacher__

If a dog eats grass, she is sick.

Circle every dog that is sick.

57

Name_____

1. What is the name of the genie in this story? __Ott__

2. Was that genie very good at genie tricks? __no__

3. What was the name of the girl who found the yellow bottle? __Carla__

4. What street was she on? __Bide__

5. How many boys began to follow Carla? __three__ (or **3**)

6. Did the boys think there was a genie in the bottle? __no__

7. Did Carla really think there was a genie in the bottle? __no__

8. Who came out of the bottle when Carla rubbed it? __Ott__

★★★★★★★★★★★★★★★★★★★★★★★★★★★★★★★★

1. Did Sid send out pine trees or pin trees? __pin trees__ (p.20)

2. What did the boss keep in her cane can? __her cane__ (p.19)

3. What did Sid make for the window? __a pan__ (p.20)

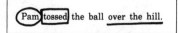

(Pam) (tossed) the ball over the hill.

1. Make a box around the word tossed.

2. Circle the word that tells who tossed the ball.

3. Make a line under the words that tell where she tossed the ball.

Once there was a bit of ice in an icebox. "It is cold in this icebox," the bit of ice said. "I will go where it is hot."

"If you go where it is hot you will melt," the other bits of ice said. But the bit of ice went to where it was hot. It wasn't long before she saw that she was getting smaller.

"I'm melting," the bit of ice said. "I must go back in the icebox." And she did. Now she is smaller but happy.

1. This story is about a bit of __ice__ .

2. The ice lived in an ice __box__ .

3. Where did the ice want to go? where it is __hot__

4. What happened to the ice? It began to __melt__

5. Where is the bit of ice now? in the __icebox__

If a tree is bent, it is old.

Circle every tree that is old.

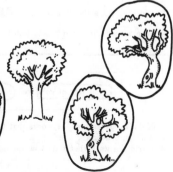

1. Who said, "Oh, master Carla, what can I do for you"? __Ott__
2. Who said, "Give those boys a spanking"? __Carla__
3. Did Ott give the boys a spanking or a banking? a __banking__
4. Ott told Carla that he was a very __old__ genie.
5. Was that a lie? __yes__
6. Did Ott send Carla back home or to Rome? __to Rome__
7. What is the title of this story?
   __Ott Tells Lies__

★★★★★★★★★★★★★★★★★★★★★★★★★★★★★★★

1. What did the tiger have in his pouch? __stones__ (p.38)
   cash   stones   rocks   tigers
2. What did he get from the man at the stand?
   __ice cream cone and string__ (p.39)
3. He made the cone into a __hat__ . (p.39)

> The genie looked (small).

1. Make a w over the word looked.
2. Circle the word that tells how the genie looked.
3. Make a line under the words that tell what looked small.

58

A mean man had a bottle with a genie in it. Every day the mean man made the genie do tricks. But the mean man never liked the tricks. One day the mean man said, "I am tired of seeing you make gold appear. Let's see your best trick."

"Yes, master," the genie said. "I will show you my very best trick."

The genie waved his hands and turned the mean man into a log.

1. Who had the bottle? __a mean man__
2. Did the mean man like the genie's tricks? __no__
3. Who said, "I will show you my very best trick"? __the genie__
4. What did the man turn into? __a log__

> If a man is tired, he is sitting.

Circle every man that is tired.

1. What is the title of this story?
   __Ott Is a Very Sad Genie__
2. Where did Ott send Carla from the bank? to __Rome__
   a spanking   her home   Rome   genie school
3. Where did they go from Rome? to __a forest__
   Carla's home   a forest   a lake   a bank
4. Did Ott make an alligator or an apple? an __alligator__
5. Did Ott make a peach or a beach? a __beach__
6. Who said, "You are a mess of a genie"? __Carla__
7. Did Ott make a hot log or a hot dog? a __hot log__
8. Was Ott happy or sad? __sad__

★★★★★★★★★★★★★★★★★★★★★★★★★★★★★★★

1. What did the ghosts get from the monster? __her gold rod__ (p.70)
2. Did they scare the monster? __yes__ (p.70)
3. Who turned the mean ghosts into happy ghosts? __Boo__ (p.75)

> That pile of gold feels (cold).

1. Make a box around the words that tell what feels cold.
2. Make a p over the word feels.
3. Circle the word that tells how the pile of gold feels.

One day Spot met Boo the ghost. Boo had a magic rod. Spot said, "I want some bones. What do I say to make bones appear?"

Boo told Spot to hold the rod and say, "Hope, bone, bone, hope."

Spot tried to say that. But what she said was, "Home, cone, cone, home." When Spot said those words, she saw that she could fly like a bird. Now she has fun flying.

1. Who did Spot meet? __Boo__
2. What did Boo have? a magic __rod__
3. What did Spot want? __some bones__
4. Spot said, "Home, cone, __cone__ , __home__ ."
5. Did Spot make bones appear? __no__

> Every fat bird likes bugs.

Circle every bird that likes bugs.

1. Ott said, "I will make a sound that is very ___loud___ ."

2. Did Ott make a sound that was loud? __no__

3. What did he make? a ___cloud___

4. When Ott tried to make a cloud, he made a ___loud___ sound.

5. Who gave Ott a kiss? __Carla__

6. When Ott wished them to go home, where did they go? ___to Rome___

7. Who said, "I don't know how I do that"? ___Ott___

8. What is the title of this story?

___Carla and Ott Can't Get Home___

★★★★★★★★★★★★★★★★★★★★★★★★★★★

1. Dan was a ___dog___ . (p.34)

2. What was the name of the dog that helped the teacher? __Dan__ (p.36)

3. Could that dog read well? __yes__ (p.34)

4. Did the boys and girls come to class early or late? __early__ (p.37)

```
[This elephant] sounds (loud).
```

1. Circle the word that tells how the elephant sounds.

2. Make a line under the word <u>sounds</u>.

3. Make a box around the words that tell what sounds loud.

There was an alligator that liked to eat things. She ate a tiger. She ate a monster. She ate anything that got in her way. Ten bugs got in her way. She ate them. They tickled inside the alligator. When the alligator opened her mouth to laugh, all the animals came out. The tiger, the monster, and the ten bugs all came out. Now everybody is happy but the alligator.

1. What did the alligator like to do? ___eat things___

2. Who tickled her? __ten bugs__

3. Did the bugs come out? __yes__

4. Did the monster come out? __yes__

5. Is the alligator happy now? __no__

> Every white box is made of wood.

Circle all the wood boxes.

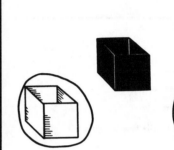

59

---

1. What was streaming down Carla's cheek? a ___tear___

2. Where were Ott and Carla? in ___Rome___

3. Did Ott tell Carla that he had lied to her? ___yes___

4. Who tried to call for help? ___Ott___

5. What hit Ott in the face? a ___fish___
   dish   fish   hot dog   beach

6. Who said, "I wish you would get out of here"? ___Carla___

7. Where did the bottle go when Carla tossed it? ___through a window___
   crash   through a window   on the ground   fast

★★★★★★★★★★★★★★★★★★★★★★★★★★★

1. Who began to howl when the ghosts got near the castle? ___the hounds___ (p.69)
   the monster   the hounds   the horse

2. Who was sitting at the table when the ghosts floated in? ___the monster___ (p.69)
   Boo   the monster   the boss

3. Which ghost could read what it said on the magic rod? __Boo__ (p.75)

```
      b
A car rolled down the hill.
```

1. Make a <u>b</u> over the word <u>down</u>.
2. Make a <u>line</u> under the words that tell where the car rolled.
3. Make a line over the words that tell what rolled down the hill.

A girl had six apples. These apples were in her house. The con fox had a plan for getting the apples. He made a big swing near the house. He got on the swing and began to swing very hard. Then he let go and went flying into the girl's house. But he landed in a tub. The girl picked him up and said, "What are you doing in here? You're all wet." So she put him on the line to dry. That con fox is not happy.

1. Who made a swing? ___the con fox___

2. What was the fox trying to get? ___six apples___

3. What did he land in? ___a tub___

4. Who hung him on the line? ___the girl___

5. Why did she put the fox on the line? ___to dry___

> All the old coats are Bob's.

Circle every coat that is Bob's.

1. Who went back into the yellow bottle? __Ott__

2. Who came running from the house? __a woman__

      a woman   Ott   a man   Carla

3. The woman said that __Carla__ tossed the bottle through the window.

      Ott   an old genie   Carla

4. Who was going to spank Carla? __the woman__

5. Who rubbed the bottle? __Carla__

6. Ott fixed the __pane__ of glass in the window.

      pan   pane   pine   pin

7. Who said, "Please don't hate me"? __Ott__

★★★★★★★★★★★★★★★★★★★★★★★★★★★★★★

1. Don wanted to be a __super__ man. (p.219 – Storybook 1)

2. Where did Don work? in a __hat__ shop (p.219 – Storybook 1)

3. When Don turned into a super man, he had a __cape__

and a __cap__. (p.1)

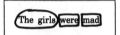

The girls were mad

1. Circle the words that tell who was mad.

2. Make a box around the word were.

3. Make a box around the word that tells how the girls felt.

60

    There was a fat cloud. That cloud was so fat that it could not keep up with the other clouds. The fat cloud became very sad and started to cry. When it cried, big drops of rain fell from the cloud. The cloud got smaller and smaller. Soon the cloud was not fat any more. Now the cloud can keep up with the other clouds.

1. The cloud was __fat__.

2. Is the cloud fat now? __no__

3. Why did the cloud cry? because it could not __keep__

__up__ with the other clouds

4. When the cloud cried, it got s__maller__.

Every girl can read well.

Circle every child who can read well.

---

1. What is the title of this story?

__Carla Reads the Genie Book__

2. Where were Ott and Carla? in __Rome__

3. What did Ott get when he called for help? a __fish__

      hot dog   pane   peach   fish

4. Carla and Ott went to the park and sat in the __shade__.

      shad   shade   home   stone

5. Carla found part of the book that said, "How to go __home__."

      Rome   bone   home   stone

6. Who began to read the book out loud? __Carla__

★★★★★★★★★★★★★★★★★★★★★★★★★★★★★★

1. Who scared the monster from the castle?

the mean __ghosts__ (p.70)

2. The monster made Boo have a fish tail and a __fin__ (p.64)

3. The monster had turned the king into a __frog__ (p.58)

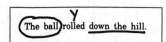

y

The ball rolled down the hill.

1. Circle the words that tell what rolled down the hill.
2. Make a y over the word rolled.
3. Make a line under the words that tell where the ball rolled.

    Jill was a horse with big, big feet. The other horses laughed at Jill. "Ho, ho," they said. "How can you run with those big feet?"
    Then it began to rain a lot. The ground became mud. One horse tried to run in the mud but he got stuck. Another horse got stuck. So did another horse. Then Jill ran in the mud. But she did not get stuck. Her feet were too big to get stuck in the mud. The other horses said, "I wish I had big feet." Jill was happy.

1. What did Jill have? __big, big feet__

2. Did the other horses get stuck in the mud? __yes__

3. Did Jill get stuck in the mud? __no__

4. Who said, "I wish I had big feet"?

__the other horses__

Every small window has glass in it.

Circle every window with glass in it.

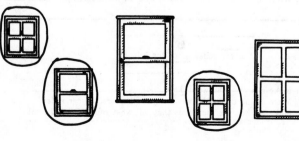

Make a line under the answer.

1. Carla was _____ from Ott's school book.
   <u>reading</u>   sitting   laughing

Fill in the blanks.

2. Carla said, "Ib, bub, ib, bub, ib, bub, bibby. Bome, **bome** , **bome** . I want to go **home** , **home** , **home** ."

3. Who said, "That is too much to remember"? **Ott**

Circle the answer.

4. Who sent Carla home?
   an old genie   (**Carla**)   Ott

Fill in the blanks.

5. Did Ott go to Carla's home? **no**

6. Who said, "I better call for help"? **Carla**

★★★★★★★★★★★★★★★★★★★★★★★★★★★★★★★★★★★★★★

Fill in the blanks.

1. Who ran around and made a hole in the school? **Don**

2. What stopped in front of the school? **a truck** (p.8)
   a bus   a truck   a tree

3. Who was in the truck? a little **man** (p.14)

4. Who said, "You are too small for this job"? **Don** (p.14)

If a cup has spots, it is hot.

Circle every cup that is hot.

There was a king who was very rich. So he had everything made out of gold. He had gold tables. He had gold lamps. He even had a gold bed. One day it got very cold out, so he put on his gold hat. Then he put on his gold boots and his gold pants. But he had so much gold on that he could not walk. He is still standing there in his gold things.

Fill in the blanks.

1. The king was very **rich** .

2. What were his things made of? **gold**

3. Who put on a gold hat? **the king**

4. Could the king walk with all those gold things on? **no**

61

Circle the answer.

1. Carla was reading the part of the book that told how to call for _____ .
   home   hounds   horses   (**help**)

Fill in the blanks.

2. What is the title of this story?
   Carla Calls for Help

3. Did a fish drop from the sky when Carla called for help? **no**

4. Did the old genie believe that Carla had called for help? **no**

5. What did the old genie hold on her head? a **rock**
   rod   rock   rag   Ron

6. Did Carla turn it into water? **yes**

Make a line under the answer.

7. Who got mad?
   Ott   <u>the old genie</u>   Carla

Fill in the blanks.

8. Who said, "I need your help"? **Carla** **Ott**

9. Who did Carla want to find? **Ott**

★★★★★★★★★★★★★★★★★★★★★★★★★★★★★★★★★★★★

Fill in the blanks.

1. How many ghosts lived with Boo? **five** (p.54) **(or 5)**

2. Were they nice to Boo? **no** (p.55)

3. Who said, "I have found somebody you can't scare"? **Boo** (p.66)

If a boy has a hat on, he is cold.

Make a box around every boy who is cold.

Edna was an old lady who could not laugh. Her brother took her to funny shows. But she did not laugh. Then one day, she met a bug. The bug said, "My friends and I can make you laugh." "No, you can't," Edna said. "Nothing can make me laugh."
So one hundred bugs came over. Ninety bugs sat on the old lady. And ten bugs tickled her and tickled her. She laughed and laughed and laughed.

Circle the answer.

1. What couldn't the old lady do?   go to shows   sit   (**laugh**)

2. Who took her to shows?   her mother   (**her brother**)   her bugs

Fill in the blanks.

3. Who said, "My friends and I can make you laugh"? **a bug**

4. Who said, "No, you can't"? **Edna**

5. Did the bugs make her laugh? **yes**

Fill in the blanks.

1. What is the title
of this story? **Carla Goes to Genie School**

2. Did the old genie say that
humans can't do very simple tricks? **yes**

Circle the answers.

3. Who said, "I will try to send another genie"?
(the old genie)   Carla   Ott

4. Who was she talking to?   **(Carla)**   Ott   the teacher

Fill in the blanks.

5. Who said, "I don't want another genie"? **Carla**

Make a line over the answers.

6. Which genie did Carla want?
the old genie   **Ott**   the teacher

7. Did the old genie let Carla go to genie school?
Yes   No

If a boy is hungry, he is jumping.

Make a box around every boy who is hungry.

62

Fill in the blanks.

1. **What is the title of this story?**
Carla Is the Best in Genie School

2. When Carla snapped her fingers, a **rock** appeared.

3. She told the boy to **sit** on the rock.

Make a line over the answers.

4. Then she turned the rock into _____ .
a bottle   **water**   a genie

5. Who was the best at doing tricks?
Ott   **Carla**   a little genie

6. Soon it was time for the children to take their genie _____ .
now   how   **vow**   cow

If the dog is little, he can run fast.

Make a line under every dog that can run fast.

Fill in the blanks.

1. One note from the boss said, "T**ape**
the oak tree near the door."   *(p.22)*

2. Another note said, "Send a c**one** to Sam's tree farm."   *(p.22-23)*

3. Another note said, "Plant seeds on the s**lope**."
(p.25)

Viz was a very sad window. He said, "Nobody
looks at me. When people are on one side of me,
they look at things that are on the other side of
me. But they never look at me."

Then one night things got very cold. Ice
formed on Viz, the window. The next day
everybody said, "Look at the pretty window." Viz
was a proud window now.

Fill in the blanks.

1. Who was sad? **Viz**

2. Why was Viz sad? because nobody looked at **him**

Make a line over the answer.

3. What happened one night?
Things got cold.   Things got wet.   Things got hot.

Fill in the blanks.

4. What formed on that window? **ice**

5. Did people look at Viz the next day? **yes**

Every rat thinks.   Linda is a rat.

What does Linda do? **She thinks.**

Fill in the blanks.

1. A tame tiger liked ice c**ream** . *(p.38)*

2. Did the tiger have cash? **no** *(p.38)*

3. Did the tiger want a con or a cone? **a cone** *(p.39)*

A little girl was mad because she was so
small. She said, "I wish I was big. I wish I
was bigger than anybody."

Boo was hiding near the girl. He took the
magic rod and said some magic words. The girl
began to grow bigger and bigger. Soon she was
as big as a house. Then she began to cry. She
said, "I don't like to be so big. I wish I was
small again." So Boo made her small again. Now
she is happy.

Fill in the blanks.

1. Why was the girl sad? because she was so **small**

2. Who said, "I wish I was big"? **the girl**

3. Who made her get bigger and bigger? **Boo**

4. Was the girl happy when she was big? **no**

5. She said, "I **wish** I was small again."

Every dog pants.   Rob is a dog.

What does Rob do? **He pants.**

Make a line under the answers.

1. Who told the children about what a genie had to do?
   Ott   Carla   <u>the old genie</u>

2. Who began to cry?
   Ott   <u>Carla</u>   the old genie

3. Was Carla ready to forget about herself
   and do what her master told her?   Yes   <u>No</u>

Fill in the blanks.

4. Was the old genie mad at her? **no**

5. Were the other children mad at Carla? **no**

6. What is the title of this story?
   Will Carla Take the Genie Vow?

7. Did Carla take the genie vow? **no**

All of the short boys have dogs.

Make a box around every boy who has a dog.

Fill in the blanks.
1. Spot met a girl who was **tall** . (p.41)
2. The girl and Spot were going to the **mall** . (p.42)
3. The girl got a **wig** for Spot. (p.45)

There was a genie named Itt. He could not
do many genie tricks. One day he tried to make
a truck appear. But he made a trunk appear.
Then he tried to make a hot dog. But he made a
hot frog. That frog was mad. He hopped in the
pond to cool off.

Fill in the blanks.
1. What was the genie's name? **Itt**
2. What couldn't he do? many genie **tricks**
3. What did he make for a truck? **a trunk**
4. What did he make for a hot dog? **a hot frog**

Every car has doors.   Sid has a car.

What does Sid's car have? **doors**

63

Fill in the blanks.

1. What is the title of this story? **Carla and Ott Are Teachers**

2. Which genie went to a yellow
   bottle that belonged to Carla? **Ott**

3. Was Ott happy? **yes**

Make a box around the answers.

4. Who told the old genie that some new bottles had been found?
   Ott   the teacher   Carla

5. How many bottles were found?   six   five   three

Fill in the blanks.

6. Who is training genies at the school now?
   Carla and **Ott**

7. Is Ott a good teacher? **yes**

8. Carla is a good teacher because she is very **smart** .

9. Is there more to come in this story? **no**

All the girls with long hair have pets.

Make a line over the girls who have pets.

Fill in the blanks.

1. What did Ott make when he
   tried to make an apple? **an alligator** (p.81)

2. What did Ott make when he
   tried to make a peach? **a beach** (p.85)

3. Who told Ott that he would have to
   go into the yellow bottle? the old g**enie** (p.86)

Once there was a sad horse. The horse had
flies on his back. He tried to get rid of the
flies but he couldn't. The flies kept biting him
and biting him.
   At last the horse yelled, "I hate flies."
   A bird said, "I don't hate them. I love them."
The bird hopped on the horse's back and ate
the flies. Now the horse is happy and so is the bird.

Fill in the blank.
1. What did the horse have on his back? **flies**

Circle the answer.
2. Could the horse get rid of the flies?
   Yes   (No)

Make a box under the answers.
3. Who said that he loved flies?
   the bird   the farmer   the horse
       □
4. The bird _____ the flies.   kissed   ate   hugged
                                              □

Every bird eats bugs.   Ron is a bird.

What does Ron do? **He eats bugs.**

Fill in the blank.

1. Did Kim spell well? __no__

Circle the answer.

2. How did Kim spell the word <u>made</u>? (mad) mod made

Make a box around the answers.

3. How did Kim spell the word <u>van</u>? von [vane] van

4. How did Kim spell the word <u>mat</u>? mot [mate] mote

Fill in the blanks.

5. Kim wanted to look under the word ___van___ in the phone book.

6. But Kim looked under the word __vane__ .

7. The woman said that she would send the vane to Kim's house in __five__ minutes.

8. What is the title of this story? ___The Van and the Vane___

All the men with hats have red hair.

Circle the men with red hair.

64

Fill in the blanks.

1. Did Kim need a van or a vane? a ___van___

2. What did she get? a __vane__

Make a box around the answer.

3. How did Kim feel? [mad] made mate mat

Circle the answers.

4. Did Kim try to find the word <u>truck</u> or the word <u>trunk</u> in the phone book? (truck) trunk

5. Which word did she find? truck (trunk)

Fill in the blanks.

6. Did Kim have to pay for the trunk? __yes__

7. How many dollars did she have to pay? __ninety__

8. Was Kim very happy? __no__

All of the big eggs have chicks in them.

Make a box around every egg with a chick in it.

Fill in the blanks.

1. Did Ott give the mean boys a spanking? __no__ (p.90)

2. What did he give them? __a banking__ (p.90)

3. Did Ott send Carla to her home or to Rome? __to Rome__ (p.92)

There was an old clock that didn't work. The woman who had the clock said, "I will throw this old clock out. It doesn't work." So she did.

A bum looked at the clock and said, "I am a bum. I don't work. That clock doesn't work. So I will get along well with that clock."

Now the bum is happy. He doesn't work and he has a clock that doesn't work.

Make a circle under the answer.

1. Who said, "I will throw this old clock out"? the woman the clock the bum

Make a box over the answer.

2. Who found the clock? a woman a clock a bum

Fill in the blanks.

3. The bum doesn't __work__ and he has a __clock__ that doesn't __work__ .

All children go to school.   Tom and Linda are children.

What do Tom and Linda do? __They go to school.__

Fill in the blanks.

1. What did Ott make when he tried to make a hot dog? __a hot log__ (p.94)

2. What did Ott make when he tried to make an apple? __an alligator__ (p.94)

3. What did Ott make when he tried to make a peach? __a beach__ (p.94)

A snake named Bill was sad because he could not kick the ball. The other animals said, "Ho, ho. You can't kick a ball. Snakes don't have legs."

Then one day Bill went to the place where the other animals were kicking the ball. Bill said, "I can make the ball go as far as any other animal." He hit the ball with his nose. It went very far.

The other animals said, "That snake doesn't have legs, but he can really kick with his nose."

Circle the answer.

1. The snake was named _____ . Ball Bull (Bill)

Make a circle under the answer.

2. He could not _____ a ball. hit lick kick

Make a circle over the answer.

3. The other animals said, "Snakes don't have _____ ." feet legs ears

---

Every mip is an animal.   Linda has a mip.

What do you know about her mip? __It is an animal.__

Fill in the blanks.

1. What is the title of this story?

   __A Man Brings False Teeth__

2. What did Kim get when she tried to call for a van? a __vane__

3. What did Kim get when she tried to call for a truck? a __trunk__

Circle the answer.

4. What did Kim look up when she tried to find a rental car?

   dental car   rental care   (dental care)

Fill in the blanks.

5. What was Kim trying to rent from the man? a __car__

6. What did the man think Kim was trying to rent? __false teeth__

7. Was the man's name under "rental car"? __no__

Tim made all the dresses with buttons.

Circle every dress that Tim made.

Fill in the blanks.

1. When Ott tried to make a sound that was loud, he made a c__loud__. (p.96)

2. When Ott called for help, a __fish__ hit him in the face. (p.100)

3. Carla tossed a bottle through a __window__. (p.100)

There was an old bug who could do many tricks. She could drive a car. She could stand on her head. She could sing, but nobody could hear her. She was so small that nobody saw her tricks. Then one day, she drove a car into a big tent. The girl inside the tent grabbed the bug and said, "This old bug can drive cars. I will put her into my show." And she did. Now the old bug is the star of a show.

Circle the answer.

1. The bug could do _____ .

   no tricks   (many tricks)   one trick

Make a box under the answer.

2. The bug was very _____ .   sick   small   big
                                          □

Make a box over the answer.

3. Who grabbed the bug? the girl inside the _____
                              □
                           tent   house   horse

Fill in the blank.

4. Now the bug is the __star__ of a show.

Every glip is red.   Tom is a glip.

What do you know about Tom? __He is red.__

Make a line under the answers.

1. Who tossed the phone book out of the window?
   a boy   Ott   __Kim__

2. Who picked up the phone book?
   a boy   Ott   Kim

Fill in the blanks.

3. Who found the phone number for a van? __a boy__

4. Who said, "Can I go with you?" __a boy__

Make a box around the answers.

5. Did the boy lead Kim to Jane Street or Jan Street?
   Jan Street   [Jane Street]

6. Could that boy read very well?
   [Yes]   No

7. What did Kim give the boy?
   [a vane]   dental care   a van

Jill made all the dresses with buttons.

Circle every dress that Jill made.

Fill in the blanks.

1. Carla told the old genie to hold a __rock__ on her head. (p.111)

2. Did the old genie get wet? __yes__ (p.111)

3. Did Carla take her genie vow? __no__ (p.120)

The con fox said, "I want some honey. But every time I take some honey from the bees, the bees chase me away. I need to trick the bees."

The con fox called, "Oh, bees. There are flowers by the stream. Why don't you go to those flowers?"

The bees said, "That silly fox thinks he can fool us. He wants our honey." The bees chased the fox away.

Circle the answer.

1. The con fox wanted _____ .   bees   birds   (honey)

Make a box around the answer.

2. The fox tried to _____ the bees.   [trick]   eat   find

Fill in the blanks.

3. He told them about some flowers near the __stream__ .

4. Did the trick work? __no__

Every tiger is mean.   Zag is a tiger.

What do you know about Zag? __He is mean.__

Fill in the blank.

1. What is the title of this story?

   Ellen the Eagle

Circle the answers.

2. What did Ellen's brother need?

   (water)   food   a bed

3. What was in the bottom of the hole?

   (water)   food   Ellen's brother

Fill in the blanks.

4. Was the hole very wide? **no**

5. Ellen and her brother dropped stones into the **hole** .

6. Did the stones make the water go up or down? **up**

7. Did Ellen and her brother drink water? **yes**

All of the white horses can run fast.

Circle every horse that can run fast.

66

Fill in the blanks.

1. How many mean ghosts lived with Boo? **five**   (p.54)

2. The monster had made the king into a **frog** . (p.58)

3. The monster had a gold **rod** . (p.61)

Once there was a chicken that wanted to be a fox. It would chase all the other chickens, jump at them, and yell at them. All the other chickens would run away saying, "That chicken is a nut."

One day a real fox came along. The real fox saw the chicken and said, "What are you?"

The chicken said, "I am a fox."

The fox said, "I think I will eat this fox." The fox began to chase the chicken.

The chicken said, "I am tired of being a fox. I will be a chicken now." And the chicken flew away.

Make a box around the answers.

1. What did the chicken want to be?   [a fox]   a box   a man

2. Who did the chicken meet?   a boy   [a fox]   a box

Fill in the blanks.

3. Who said, "I think I'll eat this fox"? **the fox**

4. Who said, "I am tired of being a fox"? **the chicken**

Every boy has long pants.   Bob is a boy.

What does Bob have? **long pants**

Make a line under the answers.

1. Carl was a _____ .

   ran   <u>mouse</u>   cat

2. The other mice wanted something to _____ .

   drink   look at   <u>eat</u>

Circle the answer.

3. Who went out to find food for the other mice?

   (Carl)   Fred   a crow

Fill in the blanks.

4. Who did Carl see? **a crow**

5. What did the crow have in his mouth?

   a very big chunk of cheese

6. Did Carl get the cheese? **yes**

Every man with a hat will go fishing.

Circle every man that will go fishing.

Fill in the blanks.

1. The old genie told the teacher that a girl had found a **bottle** . (p.82)

2. Did the teacher think that Ott should go to the bottle? **no** (p.86)

3. What did Ott make when he tried to make a loud sound? **a cloud** (p.96)

Chickens are not the only animals that lay eggs. A chicken is a bird, and all birds lay eggs. So do snakes and alligators. Turtles and fish lay eggs too. Did you know that ants and other bugs lay eggs? The egg holds the baby animal. A baby turtle comes out of an egg. And a baby snake comes out of an egg. Baby chickens come from the kind of eggs that you eat.

Make a box under the answer.

1. Are chickens the only animals that lay eggs?   Yes   No [ ]

Make a line over the answer.

2. All _____ lay eggs.   rabbits   <u>birds</u>   monkeys

Fill in the blank.

3. What does an egg hold? a baby **animal**

Circle the answer.

4. What is the best title for this story?

   Chickens Lay Eggs   (Animals That Lay Eggs)   The Baby Snake

Every crow likes bugs.   Jane is a crow.

What does Jane like? **bugs**

Fill in the blanks.

1. What is the title of this story?

   The Turtle and the Frog

2. Who grabbed a fly and ate it? the turtle

Make a box around the answer.

3. Who jumped way up?

   a turtle   a snake   a frog

Fill in the blanks.

4. Did the turtle jump way up? no

5. Was the frog nice to the turtle? no

Circle the answer.

6. Did the turtle feel happy or sad?

   happy   sad

Every big box has kittens in it.

Circle every box with kittens in it.

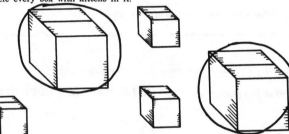

Fill in the blanks.

1. Who planted seeds in the slop? Sid (p.26)

2. Who told Sid, "I will teach you to read"? the boss (p.31)

3. Did the boss teach Sid to read well? yes (p.32)

A weed is a plant that people don't want. In some parts of the world, a rose is called a weed. We think a rose is a pretty flower. But it is a weed when it grows where nobody wants it. And we like some plants that grow like weeds in other parts of the world.

Fill in the blanks.

1. A weed is a plant that people don't want .

2. Could a pretty flower be a weed? yes

3. Could a big plant be a weed? yes

4. A plant that you buy is not a weed .

5. Could a rose be a weed? yes

Every house has windows.   I made a house.

What do you know about the house I made?

It has windows.

Circle the answers.

1. What was Flame?

   a woman   a snake   a frog

2. Could the turtle do things the frog could do?

   Yes   No

Fill in the blanks.

3. What is the title of this story?

   Flame the Snake

4. Who told the turtle that he looked like a toenail? the frog

Make a line under the answer.

5. Who was looking for frogs?

   a turtle   a snake   a frog

Fill in the blank.

6. Did the turtle tell a lie to the snake? yes

Jane will buy every bottle that is little and round.

Circle every bottle that Jane will buy.

Fill in the blanks.

1. Did Ott give the mean boys a spanking or a banking? a banking (p.90)

2. What did Ott make when he tried to make a hot dog? a hot log (p.94)

3. Where did Ott send Carla when he tried to send her home? to Rome (p.92)

Some caves are holes under the ground. Some caves are small and some are big. Small animals like to sleep in caves that are on the side of mountains. Some caves are very big. In one big cave you could walk for over 80 miles. You could walk for days and days and not see every part of the cave. And you would never see the sun while you were in that cave. The cave is under the ground and things are very dark there.

Fill in the blanks.

1. Some caves are big holes under the ground .

2. Are all caves big? no

3. If you were in a big cave would you see the sun? no

4. In one big cave you could walk for over 80 miles.

5. In that cave, you could walk for days and days .

Every bottle is made of glass.   I have a bottle.

What do you know about the bottle I have?

It is made of glass.

Circle the answer.

1. Did the turtle lie to the snake? (Yes) No

Fill in the blanks.

2. What's the title of this story? **Flame the Snake Is a Sneak**

3. Was Flame fast? **yes**

4. Was Flame a sneak? **yes**

Make a box around the answers.

5. Where did the frog jump when Flame was chasing him?
   [into the weeds]   into the pond   into a tree

6. Who said, "I'll bite you on the nose"?
   the frog   the snake   [the turtle]

Fill in the blank.

7. Did the snake try to bite the turtle? **yes**

Every dog with long ears is named Sandy.

Circle every dog named Sandy.

Fill in the blanks.

1. Kim could not **spell** well. (p.125)   (p.125)

2. What did Kim get when she tried to phone for a van? **a vane**

3. What did Kim get when she tried to phone for a truck? **a trunk**
   (p.128)

Trees have roots. The roots are under the ground. The roots hold the tree up and keep it from falling over. The roots also carry water from the ground to the tree. So the roots do two things. They hold the tree up and they bring water to the tree. Trees could not live if they did not have roots.

Fill in the blanks.

1. All trees have **roots** .

2. Where are the roots? under the **ground**

3. How many things do the roots do? **two (or 2)**

4. They keep the tree from **falling** over.

5. They bring **water** to the tree.

6. Could trees live if they didn't have roots? **no**

Every girl has a short dress.   Terry is a girl.

What do you know about her? **She has a short dress.**

Fill in the blanks.

1. What is the title of this story? **A Snake Must Do What Snakes Do**

2. Did Flame try to bite the turtle? **yes**

Make a line under the answers.

3. Flame hit her tooth on the turtle's _____ .
   nose   shell   ear

4. Flame said, "I think I broke my _____ ."
   nose   shell   tooth

Fill in the blanks.

5. Did the turtle let Flame go after the frog? **yes**

6. Was the turtle happy? **no**

Ann has all the dogs with spots.

Circle every dog that Ann has.

Fill in the blanks.

1. Did Kim think she called for a rental car or for dental care? **a rental car**   (p.132)

2. Who helped Kim call for a van? **a boy** (p.135)

3. What did Kim give the boy for helping her? **a vane** (p.137)

Some caves are big holes under the ground. Animals live in some of the big caves. These animals are fish and bugs. They spend all their time in the dark. They never see the sun. And they are very strange. Most of them are white. They cannot see because they never have to use their eyes. Remember the two ways that they are strange: they cannot see, and they are white.

Fill in the blanks.

1. The animals that live in big caves are **fish** and **bugs** .

2. What color are most of these animals? **white**

3. Can these animals see? **no**

4. These animals never see the **sun** .

5. Is it light or dark in the big caves? **dark**

6. So do these animals need eyes that see? **no**

All kites are red.   Mom has a kite.

What do you know about her kite? **It is red.**

Make a line over the answers.

1. Who slid into the weeds?

    the turtle   <u>the snake</u>   the frog

2. Who bit the snake?

    <u>the turtle</u>   the snake   the frog

Fill in the blanks.

3. Where did the frog hide? __in the weeds__

4. Could he jump well in the weeds? __no__

Circle the answers.

5. Did the frog come out of the weeds?   (Yes)   No

6. Does Flame go after the frog any more?   Yes   (No)

Ted made every coat that is white.

Circle every coat that Ted made.

Fill in the blanks.

1. Did Ellen and her brother take a train or fly? __fly__ (p.138)

2. What did Ellen's brother need? __water__ (p.138)

3. What did the eagles drop into the hole? __stones__ (p.139)

Once there was a frog that liked to stick to things. One day, the frog said, "I will stick to this log." But the frog did not stick to a log. The frog stuck to an alligator's nose.

The alligator said, "I will open my mouth and the frog will fall in." The alligator opened her mouth. The frog did not fall in. The frog just stuck to the alligator's nose.

The frog said, "I like this log. It goes up and down. I will stick here all day." And he did.

Fill in the blanks.

1. Who liked to stick to things? __a frog__

2. Did the frog stick to a log? __no__

3. He stuck to an alligator's __nose__ .

Circle the answers.

4. Who opened her mouth?   a frog   (an alligator)   a log

5. Did the frog like to stick on the alligator's nose?   (Yes)   No

Fill in the blanks.

6. The alligator's nose went __up__ and __down__ .

All rabbits hop.   Al has a rabbit.

What does Al's rabbit do? __It hops.__

Make a box around the answer.

1. The boy watched _____ .

    mountain lions   wolves   [sheep]

Fill in the blanks.

2. What's the title of this story?

__The Boy Who Yelled "Wolf"__

3. Was the boy a hard worker? __no__

Circle the answer.

4. Who yelled "Wolf" when there was no wolf?

    the lion   (the boy)   the sheep

Fill in the blanks.

5. Did a real wolf come after the sheep? __yes__

6. Did the people in the town believe the boy? __no__

7. Was the boy good at his job after that? __yes__

Every bug with a tail is a zerm.

Circle every zerm.

Fill in the blanks.

1. The other mice sent Carl out for __food__ . (p.141)

2. Who did Carl see in a tree? __a crow__ (p.141)

3. What did that crow have in his mouth? __cheese__ (p.141)

Pat was a bug that could fly. But Pat did not fly. She swam. The other bugs said, "You should not be swimming. You should be flying."

Just then a flock of birds came over head. One of the bugs said, "We cannot stay here. The birds will get us. We will fly."

Pat said, "If you fly, a bird will eat you. Follow me." And she went into the water. So all the bugs swam away. They were safe from the birds.

Now the bugs say, "Pat is right. It is fun to swim."

Circle the answer.

1. Pat liked to _____ .   fly   talk   (swim)

Fill in the blank.

2. Who said, "You should be flying"? __the other bugs__

Make a line under the answer.

3. A flock of _____ came over.   <u>birds</u>   sheep   bugs

Fill in the blank.

4. Did the bugs fly away or swim away? __swim__ away

All cookies are sweet.   Ann has a cookie.

What do you know about Ann's cookie? __It is sweet.__

Make a line over the answers.

1. Who said, "I am so fast that nobody can beat me in a race"?
   <u>the rabbit</u>   the owl   the turtle

2. Who said, "I will race with you"?
   the rabbit   the owl   <u>the turtle</u>

Fill in the blanks.

3. Did the rabbit say she would stop saying
   how fast she was if she didn't win the race? __yes__

4. Did the rabbit and the turtle plan to
   have a long race or a short race? __a long race__

5. Who said "Go" at the start of the race? __the owl__

6. Who went down the path like a
   shot, the rabbit or the turtle? __the rabbit__

Roy will smell every little flower.

Circle every flower that Roy will smell.

70

Make a box around the answers.

1. The other animals wanted the _____ to win the race.
   owl   [turtle]   rabbit

2. But the _____ went down the path like a shot.
   owl   turtle   [rabbit]

Fill in the blanks.

3. Who stopped to rest under a big tree? __the rabbit__

4. Did the rabbit go to sleep? __yes__

5. Who said, "I'll just keep going"? __the turtle__

Circle the answers.

6. Who said, "Come on, turtle"?
   the rabbit   the turtle   (the other animals)

7. Did the rabbit win the race?   Yes   (No)

Linda made all of the big cakes.

Circle all the cakes Linda made.

Fill in the blanks.

1. Where did Kim want to move? To the other __side of town__ (p.125)

2. Did Kim want a van or a vane? __a van__ (p.125)

3. Did Kim want a truck or a trunk? __a truck__ (p.128)

4. Did Kim want dental care or a rental car? __a rental car__ (p.132)

    There was a fox who liked to steal food. He
would wait for one of the other animals to get some
food. Then the fox would scare the animal away
and eat the food. All the animals were mad at him.
    One day a mouse said, "I will stop that fox from
stealing." The mouse hid a hot pepper in some food.
The fox scared the mouse away from the food.
Then the fox ate the food. The fox jumped around
and ran around and yelled, "My mouth is on fire."
Now the fox does not steal food from the other animals.

Fill in the blank.

1. Who liked to steal food? __a fox__

Make a line over the answer.

2. Who stopped him from stealing?
   the fox   <u>the mouse</u>   the alligator

Circle the answer.

3. What did the mouse leave for the fox?
   (a pepper)   an apple   an alligator

All pips are good to eat.   Jane ate a pip.

What do you know about the pip Jane ate?
__It is good to eat.__

Fill in the blanks.

1. Flame hit her tooth on the turtle's __shell__ (p.155)

2. Did the turtle let Flame go after the frog? __yes__ (p.156)

3. Could the frog jump well in the weeds? __no__ (p.152)

    The tall man always went to sleep in the bed.
But he made his dog sleep on the floor. The dog
said, "I must use my head, head, head and find a
way to get in bed, bed, bed."
    So the dog jumped up and yelled. "I hear a
wolf in the yard." The tall man ran after the wolf.
The dog locked the door and said, "Now that I
locked the door, door, door, I won't sleep on the
floor, floor, floor."

Make a circle over the answer.

1. The tall man made the dog sleep on _____.
   the floor   the bed   the mat

Make a box under the answer.

2. The tall man went to sleep _____.
   on the floor   in the bed   on a mat

Fill in the blanks.

3. Who said, "I hear a wolf in the yard"? __the dog__

4. Who went after the wolf? __the tall man__

All rats have teeth.   Dan has two rats.

What do you know about Dan's rats? __They have teeth.__

Fill in the blank.

1. What is the title of this story?

The Lion and the Mouse

Make a line over the answers.

2. Who said, "I want to be your friend"?

the rabbit   the lion   <u>the mouse</u>

3. Who said, "I am the king of all the animals"?

the rabbit   <u>the lion</u>   the mouse

Fill in the blanks.

4. What did the lion get in his paw? <u>a big thorn</u>

5. Could the elephant get the thorn? <u>no</u>

6. Could the alligator get the thorn? <u>no</u>

7. Who got the thorn? <u>the mouse</u>

8. Are the lion and the mouse good friends now? <u>yes</u>

Every big fish likes bugs.

Circle every fish that likes bugs.

Fill in the blanks.

1. How many mean ghosts lived with Boo? <u>five</u> (p.54)

2. Which ghost could read the words on the gold rod? <u>Boo</u> (p.75)

3. Are the people in Boo's town afraid of ghosts now? <u>no</u> (p.80)

The tall man went riding on his bike. His dog ran next to him. The dog said, "I would like, like, like to ride that bike, bike, bike." But the tall man would not let the dog ride his bike.

Soon the man stopped to talk to his friends. The dog jumped on the bike and started to ride. He saw a tree. He tried to ride around it, but the bike hit the tree. The dog fell to the ground. The dog said, "I do not like, like, like to ride a bike, bike, bike."

Fill in the blanks.

1. The tall <u>man</u> went riding on his <u>bike</u>.

Make a box over the answer.

2. Did the tall man let the dog ride the bike?   Yes   ☐ No

Fill in the blanks.

3. Why did the man stop riding? <u>to talk to friends</u>

4. Who jumped on the bike? <u>the dog</u>

5. What did the dog hit? a <u>tree</u>

All dogs have bones.   Spot is a dog.

So what does Spot have? <u>bones</u>

71

Make a box around the answers.

1. What was Casey?

a lion   a fox   a mouse   [a rabbit]

2. Which animal liked to steal hens from a barn?

a lion   [a fox]   a mouse   a rabbit

Fill in the blanks.

3. What is the title of this story? <u>Casey the Rabbit</u>

4. Who would chase the fox into the lake? <u>the bees</u>

Make a line over the answers.

5. What did the fox put out for Casey to eat?

<u>a salad</u>   a hen   a rabbit

6. Casey said, "Don't throw me into the _____."

thorn trees   <u>thorn bushes</u>   lake

7. Casey said, "I'm Casey the rabbit, and you can't _____ me."

thorn   <u>hurt</u>   kill   kiss

If a boy is tall and smiling, he has a brother.

Circle every boy who has a brother.

Fill in the blanks.

1. Who said, "I am so fast that nobody can beat me in a race"? <u>the rabbit</u> (p.165)

2. Who said, "I will race with you"? <u>the turtle</u> (p.165)

3. Could the turtle run as fast as the rabbit? <u>no</u> (p.168)

An ant is an insect. A fly is an insect. A butterfly is an insect. A grasshopper is an insect, Is a spider an insect? No. A spider looks like other insects, but it is not an insect. The body of any insect has three parts. The body of an ant has three parts. The body of a butterfly has three parts. But the body of a spider does not have three parts. So a spider is not an insect.

Fill in the blanks. (any three)

1. Name three insects. <u>ant, fly, butterfly, grasshopper</u>

2. How many parts does the body of an insect have? <u>three</u>

3. How many parts does the body of an ant have? <u>three</u>

4. Is a spider an insect? <u>no</u>

5. Why isn't a spider an insect? <u>The body of a spider does not have three parts.</u>

Every table has legs.   I have a table.

What do you know about my table? <u>It has legs.</u>

Fill in the blanks.

1. What is the title of this story? **Mr. Hall**

2. What was Mr. Hall afraid of? **dogs**

3. Was he more afraid of big dogs or little dogs? **big dogs**

Circle the answers.

4. Mr. Hall went on a _____.   hill   dog   (ship)

5. Where was he going?

(to Japan)   to the U.S.   to Rome

Make a line over the answer.

6. What did he see on the deck of the ship?

a snake   a dog   a bike

Fill in the blanks.

7. Did the ship sink? **yes**

8. Did Mr. Hall find a raft or a life boat? **a raft**

9. Who swam closer and closer to him? **a dog**

There is a dog behind every box that has toys in it.

Circle every box that has a dog behind it.

72

Fill in the blanks.

1. Ott went to a school for **genies** . (p.81)

2. Carla found a yellow **bottle** . (p.87)

3. How many teachers are now teaching in the genie school? **two** (p.123)

4. What are their names? **Carla and Ott** (p.123)

People once believed the world was flat. They said, "If you sail to the end of the sea you will fall off."

One man said, "I think the world is round. I think I could sail all the way around the world without falling off." The man got a big ship and many men. He went on a long trip in that ship. He found a new land that people didn't know about. The name of that place is America.

Fill in the blanks.

1. Long ago, people used to think the world was **flat**

2. One man said, "I think the world is **round** ."

3. Is the world round or flat? **round**

Every rimp is an animal.   Jane has a rimp.

What do you know about her rimp? **It is an animal.**

Make a box around the answers.

1. After the ship went down, Mr. Hall found a _____.

boat   bike   [raft]

2. What swam to his raft?   [a dog]   a goat   a man

Circle the answers.

3. Did Mr. Hall sit near the dog?   Yes   (No)

4. What did Mr. Hall toss to the dog?

meat   (crackers)   dog food   a snake

5. What came near the raft?

a bike   a raft   a man   (a ship)

Fill in the blanks.

6. Could the people hear Mr. Hall? **no**

7. Who could they hear? **the dog**

8. Does Mr. Hall like the dog now? **yes**

If a lady has long hair and a long dress, she is a mother.

Circle every mother.

Fill in the blanks.

1. Did the other animals want the rabbit or the turtle to win the race? **the turtle** (p.168)

2. Who fell asleep under the big tree? **the rabbit** (p.168)

3. Did the turtle win the race? **yes** (p.170)

There was a girl who sucked her thumb. She made loud sounds when she sucked her thumb. Her mom and dad got mad at her, but she did not stop sucking her thumb.

Then one day the dog saw her sucking her thumb. The dog said, "That thumb looks good." So when the girl put her thumb down, the dog began to lick it. Now the girl does not suck her thumb any more.

Make a circle under the answer.

1. A girl _____ her thumb.

socked   sucked   painted
        O

Make a circle over the answer.

2. Her mom and _____ got mad at her.
                    O
dog   brother   dad

Fill in the blanks.

3. Who said, "That thumb looks good"? **the dog**

4. Now the **girl** does not **suck**

her **thumb** .

All bump weeds are sweet.   Carol has a bump weed.

What do you know about her bump weed? **It is sweet.**

Circle the answer.

1. The title of this story is "The Prince _____."

    and the Girl   and the Ramp   (and the Tramp)

Fill in the blanks.

2. Who said, "Everybody loves me"? **the prince**

3. Did the prince meet a ramp or a tramp? **a tramp**

Make a box around the answer.

4. Who put on the prince's robe?

    [the tramp]   the people   the king

Fill in the blanks.

5. The prince dressed like the ___ **tramp** ___.

6. Were the people nice to the real prince? **no**

7. Who did the tramp live with at the end of the story? ___ **the prince**

If it is fat and has 4 legs, it is a ronk.

Circle every ronk.

Fill in the blanks.

1. What is the title of this story? **In the Land of Peevish Pets**

2. Who said, "Sleep hard"? **Jean**

Circle the answers.

3. Did Jean sleep hard?   (Yes)   No

4. Who did Jean meet?   a dog   (a wizard)   a lady

Fill in the blanks.

5. The wizard told her, "All ___ **little crumps** ___ are mean."

6. Did Jean see strange animals? **yes**

Make a line over the answer.

7. The name of the land in Jean's dream was "the land of _____."

    <u>peevish pets</u>   many pits   peevish pits

Circle the right rule.

8. All crumps are mean.   All little drumps are mean.

    Some little crumps are mean.   (All little crumps are mean.)

Every boy with a coat and a hat is hungry.

Circle every boy who is hungry.

Fill in the blanks.

1. Who was the king of the other animals? **the lion** (p.172)

2. Who said, "I want to be your friend"? **the mouse** (p.172)

3. What did the mouse pull from the lion's paw? **a thorn** (p.174)

Do you remember about insects? An ant is an insect. A grasshopper is an insect. A fly is an insect. All insects have a body with three parts. A spider is not an insect because a spider does not have a body with three parts. A spider's body has two parts. Here is something else about insects. All insects have six legs. Spiders do not have six legs. Spiders have 8 legs.

Fill in the blanks.

1. All insects have ___ **six** ___ legs.

2. Name three animals that have six legs. **ant grasshopper fly**

3. How many legs do spiders have? **8**

4. How many parts does a spider's body have? **two**

5. How many parts does an insect's body have? **three**

All cakes are food.   I made a cake.

What do you know about my cake? **It is food.**

73

Fill in the blanks.

1. Who said, "Don't throw me in the thorn bushes"? **Casey** (p.177)

2. Did the thorn bushes hurt Casey? **no** (p.178)

3. Casey said, "I'm Casey the rabbit and you can't **hurt** me." (p.178)

If you jumped from a ladder, you would go down. If you jumped from a plane, you would fall down. But if you were very, very far from the ground, things would not be the same. When you are very, very far from the ground, you are in space. Things don't fall in space. If you stepped from a ladder in space, you would float. You would not go down. Things do not fall in space. So there is no up or down in space.

Fill in the blanks.

1. When you are very, very far from the ground, you are in **space**.

2. Do things fall when you are near the ground? **yes**

3. Do things fall when you are in space? **no**

4. If you stepped from a ladder in space, you would **float**

5. There is no **up** or **down** in space.

All mips are green.   Mom has a mip.

What do you know about her mip? **It is green.**

Fill in the blanks.

1. What was the name of the
   land Jean was in? the land of ___peevish pets___
2. What kind of crumps are mean? ___all little crumps___
3. Who told Jean how to make
   the mean crumps go away? ___the wizard___
4. How many rules did Jean have to
   know before she could go home? ___sixteen___ (or **16**)

Make a line over the answers.

5. What did Jean say to make the <u>crumps go away</u>?
   "Away."   "Go away, away."   "Away, away."   "Get out of here."
6. Did the <u>mean</u> crump go away when Jean said that?
   <u>Yes</u>   No

Fill in the blank.

7. What is the title of this story?
   ___Jean Meets a Mean Crump___

If it has spots and two ears, it is a glim.

Circle every glim.

Fill in the blanks.

1. What was Mr. Hall afraid of? ___dogs___ (p.179)
2. Did the ship sink? ___yes___ (p.180)
3. Who got on the raft with Mr. Hall? ___a dog___ (p.182)

Once there was a hound that was very tired.
The hound did not have a place to sleep. And the
night was cold and wet. So the hound began to
howl. "Owww," he said.

He woke the people up. They got mad. They
tossed socks, hats, shoes, and coats at the hound.
They tossed things until there was a big pile of
stuff.

Then the dog said, "Now I have a place to
sleep." So the dog went to sleep in the pile of
socks, hats, shoes, and coats.

Make a box around the answer.

1. The hound was very _____.
   happy   fast   old   │tired│

Make a line under the answer.

2. But he did not have a place to _____.
   eat   hide   <u>sleep</u>

Fill in the blanks.

3. So he began to ___howl___.
4. Then the dog said, "Now I have a ___place___ to ___sleep___."

All mip food is in a can.   Dan has mip food.

What do you know about Dan's mip food? ___It is in a can.___

Fill in the blanks.

1. All ___little___ crumps are ___mean___.
2. Jean was in the land of ___peevish pets___.
3. How many rules did Jean have
   to know before she could go home? ___sixteen___ (or **16**)
4. What did she say to make mean crumps go away? ___away, away___
5. Every dusty path leads ___to the lake___.

Circle the answers.

6. Who told Jean the rule about the dusty paths?
   (a wizard)   a crump   her mother
7. The water in the lake was _____.
   (pink)   red   deep

Fill in the blanks.

8. Could Jean get away from the lake by taking a dusty path? ___no___
9. Why not? ___Every dusty path leads to the lake.___

Find out where the bugs are.

Here is the rule: Every white house has bugs.

   Kim's house is brown.
   Spot's house is white.
   Ott's house is white.
   Tim's house is red.
   Mom's house is black.

Who has a house with bugs? ___Spot___ ___Ott___

All feps are words.   Carmen has feps.

What do you know about Carmen's feps? ___They are words.___

There was a bug who couldn't run. "I will
teach you to run," a wolf said. "Move your legs
very fast."

The bug tried it. "No," the wolf said. "You are
dancing, not running. Move up and down."

The bug tried. "No," the wolf said. "You are
hopping."

The wolf showed her teeth. The bug got scared
and ran faster than any bug you have ever seen.

Fill in the blanks.

1. The ___wolf___ said, "I will teach you to ___run___."

Make a circle over the answer.

2. First the wolf told the bug to move his legs _____
   up and down   here and there   very fast (O)

Make a box under the answer.

3. Then the wolf told the bug to move _____.
   up and down (▭)   here and there   very fast

Fill in the blanks.

4. The ___bug___ got scared and ___ran___
   faster than any ___bug___ you have ever seen.

Make a line under the answers.

1. The dusty paths led right back _____.

    to the mountain   <u>to the lake</u>   to a cake

2. Before Jean could leave the land of peevish pets, she had to know _____.

    <u>sixteen rules</u>   one more rule   twenty rules

Fill in the blanks.

3. The wizard told her that every rocky path leads **to the mountain**.

4. What did Jean see all around the mountain? **crumps**

5. Who ran after Jean? **the mean crumps**

6. What did Jean say to make the mean crumps go away? **away, away**

Find out who will go to Japan.

Here is the rule: The people who are running will go to Japan.

    The boss is running.
    Ellen is running.
    Boo is sitting.
    Jean is standing.
    The turtle is not running.

Who will go to Japan? **the boss   Ellen**

All glicks are small.   Ann has a glick.

What do you know about her glick? **It is small.**

    There was a dog that said, "I hate to take a bath."
That dog had bugs. The dog said, "I hate bugs."
    One day a man said, "That dog has bugs, so I will give the dog a bath."
    The dog said, "I hate baths."
    His bugs said, "We hate baths, too."
    The man gave the dog a bath, and the bugs went away.
Now the dog says, "I like baths. They made my bugs go away."

Fill in the blanks.

1. Did the dog like baths or hate baths? **hate** baths

2. Who said, "We hate baths, too"? **his bugs**

3. Who said, "I will give the dog a bath"? **a man**

4. Why does the dog like baths now?

They made his bugs go away.

Fill in the blanks.

1. What is the title of this story?

Jean Looks for Food

2. Who told the rule about red food? **the wizard**

3. What is the rule about red food?

Red food is good to eat.

Make a line under the answers.

4. Did Jean eat the ice cream?   Yes   <u>No</u>

5. Did Jean eat the red banana?   <u>Yes</u>   No

6. Did Jean eat the white grapes?   Yes   <u>No</u>

Find out who has frogs.

Rule: There are frogs in every tin cup.

    Ellen has a tin cup.
    Ott does not have a tin cup.
    Sid has a tin cup.
    Spot does not have a tin cup.
    Boo has a tin cup.

Who has frogs? **Ellen   Sid   Boo**

All flying bats are mammals.   Fred is a flying bat.

What do you know about him? **He is a mammal.**

    Some trees have very good wood. Other trees have wood that is not so good. The good wood is made into tables and chairs and other wooden things. Do you know what happens to the wood that is not so good? It is made into paper. The next time you use some paper, remember that you are using a tree.

Fill in the blank.

1. Do all trees have very good wood? **no**

Circle the answers.

2. Good wood is made into _____.

    windows and streets   (tables and chairs)   paper

3. Wood that is not so good is made into _____.

    (paper)   tables and chairs   streets

Make a line under the answer.

4. What is the best title for this story?

    <u>Some Trees Have Good Wood</u>
    Tables and Chairs Are Made of Wood
    Paper Comes from Trees

Fill in the blanks.

1. What is the name of the land in Jean's dream? __peevish pets__

2. How many rules did she have to know before she could leave? __sixteen__ (or **16**)

3. What did Jean know about all little crumps? __They are mean.__

4. What do you do to make a mean crump go away? __say, away away__

5. What kind of path goes to the lake? __every dusty path__

6. What kind of path goes to the mountain? __every rocky path__

7. What kind of food is good to eat? __red food__

8. What happened to Jean when she ate three red bananas?
__She had red stripes all over herself.__

9. Was Jean happy or sad? __sad__

Find out which girls are sitting on a pin.

Rule: Every girl who is crying is sitting on a pin.

Ned is laughing.
Peg is not crying.
Pam is crying.
Jane is playing ball.
Linda is crying.

Which girls are sitting on a pin? __Pam   Linda__

76

| Every lion is sleepy. | Peg is a lion.
| --- |

What do you know about her? __She is sleepy.__

Did you know that glass melts? If a bottle gets very hot, it can melt. First, the bottle will become soft. When the bottle gets hotter and hotter, the glass will start to turn red. When the glass is very, very hot, it will flow like water. Watch out when glass melts. It is very, very hot.

Circle the answer.

1. The best title for this story is _____.

   (Glass Melts)   Glass Becomes Soft   A Bottle

Fill in the blanks.

2. If a bottle gets very hot, what happens first?
   It will become __soft__.

3. What color will the bottle become? __red__

4. Then the glass will flow like __water__.

5. Should you touch glass when it is melting? __no__

Make a line under the answer.

6. Does glass melt?   <u>Yes</u>   No

Fill in the blanks.

1. What's the title of this story? __Jean Wants to Get Rid of the Red Stripes__

2. What happened to Jean when she ate three red bananas? __She had red stripes all over herself.__

3. Who told Jean how to make the stripes disappear? __the wizard__

4. "If you __jump__ in the lake, the stripes __will disappear__."

5. Which path did Jean take to the lake? __the dusty path__

Find out who is going to the store.

Rule: If a boy is in the park, he is going to the store.

Jack is in the school.
Bob is in the park.
Pam is in the house.
Tom is in the park.
Ted is in the bedroom.

Who is going to the store? __Bob   Tom__

| Every cup has a handle. | I have a cup.
| --- |

What do you know about the cup I have? __It has a handle.__

A man named Isaac Newton lived a long time back. One day he was sitting under a tree. An apple dropped on his head. He began to think about that apple. He made up a rule about things. Here is his rule: "What goes up must come down."

Fill in the blanks.

1. Who was sitting under the tree? __Isaac Newton__

2. What dropped on his head? __an apple__

3. Newton made up a __rule__.

4. "What goes __up__ must come __down__."

Name _____ Worksheet **153** Side **1**

Fill in the blanks.

1. Why did Jean have red stripes? **She ate three red bananas.**

2. What did she have to do to make the stripes disappear?
jump in the lake

Circle the answers.

3. Which path did she take to the lake?

the muddy path   (the dusty path)   the rocky path

4. How many little crumps were on the path?

(five)   six   one   three

5. What did she say to make the crumps go away?

"Away, you crumps."   "Away."   ("Away, away.")

Fill in the blanks.

6. Did the stripes disappear when she jumped into the lake? **yes**

7. What color was her hair now? **white**

8. If you stand **on one foot**, the white hair will go away.

Find out who ate crackers.

Rule: The people who ate crackers are sleeping.

Jane is playing ball.
Jean is sleeping.
Tim is sleeping.
The boss is yelling at Sid.
Ellen is sleeping.

Who ate crackers? **Jean   Tim   Ellen**

Worksheet **153** Side **2**

All weeds are plants.   Marta has a weed.

What do you know about Marta's weed? **It is a plant.**

Here is a rule about all living things: All living things grow, and all living things need water. Is a tree a living thing? Yes. So you know that a tree grows, and you know that a tree needs water. A dog is a living thing. So what do you know about a dog? You know a dog grows. You know that a dog needs water. You are a living thing. Do you grow? Yes. Do you need water? Yes.

Fill in the blanks.

1. All living things **grow**.

2. All living things need **water**.

3. Is a fly a living thing? **yes**

4. Name two things you know about a fly. **A fly grows. A fly needs water.**

5. Is a dog a living thing? **yes**

6. So you know that a dog **grows**.

And you know that a dog needs **water**.

7. Is a chair a living thing? **no**

8. Does a chair need water? **no**

77

Name _____ Worksheet **154** Side **1**

Fill in the blanks.

1. What did Jean do to make the stripes disappear? **She jumped into the lake.**

2. What color was her hair after she jumped in the lake? **white**

3. What's the title of this story? **Jean Makes Her White Hair Go Away**

4. What did Jean do to make the white disappear? **She stood on one foot.**

Make a line under the answers.

5. Now Jean was _____.

big   **bald**   green   old

6. What did Jean have to do to get her hair back?

clamp her hands   **clap her hands**   clamp her teeth

Find out who has cash.

Rule: Every red bottle has cash in it.

Sandy has a red bottle.
Tom has four yellow bottles.
The boss has two red bottles.
Mom has one red bottle.
Spot has a red dish.

Who has cash? **Sandy   the boss   Mom**

Worksheet **154** Side **2**

All rits are little.   Sop is a rit.

What do you know about Sop? **He is little.**

Remember the rule about living things: All living things grow, and all living things need water. Here is another rule about all living things. All living things make babies. A tree is a living thing. A tree makes baby trees. A fish is a living thing. A fish makes baby fish. A spider is a living thing. A spider makes baby spiders. Remember the rule: All living things make babies.

Fill in all the blanks.

1. What do all living things make? **babies**

2. Is a fish a living thing? **yes**

3. So a fish makes **baby fish**.

4. Is a spider a living thing? **yes**

5. So a spider makes **baby spiders**.

6. Is a chair a living thing? **no**

7. Does a chair make baby chairs? **no**

8. Name two things you know about living things.

All living things **grow**.

All living things need **water**.

Make a box around the answers.

1. Did Jean get her hair back? [Yes] No

2. What color was her hair?
   [red] yellow striped white

Make a line under the answer.

3. A _____ animal came out of the lake.
   sitting <u>talking</u> smiling

Fill in the blanks.

4. Did the animal tell Jean the right rule about dusty paths? **no**

5. Did he tell Jean the right rule about jumping in the lake? **no**

Circle the answer.

6. What did he tell her to say so that she could have fun?
   ("Side, slide.") "Slide, slide." "Side, side."

Find out who likes monsters.

Rule: Everybody who is smiling likes monsters.

   The boss is yelling at Jan.
   Jan is very sad.
   Ellen is smiling.
   The tiger is smiling.
   Dad has a tear in his eye.

Who likes monsters? __**Ellen**__ __**the tiger**__

78

All nails are made of metal.   Ann has a nail.

What do you know about her nail? **It is made of metal.**

There once was a girl with a cold head. She said, "I need a warm hat." So she got a nice big hat. But the wind blew her hat away. The girl yelled, "My head is cold again." And she ran after her hat. She fell down in some mud. A big chunk of mud stuck to her head. The girl smiled and said, "Now my head is not cold. It is warm. This mud is better than a hat." The girl wore the mud hat for three years. Soon she had many plants growing from her hat.

Make a box over the answer.

1. The girl had a _____ head.
   cold fat big old

Fill in the blanks.

2. She said, "I __**need**__ a warm __**hat**__."

Circle the answer.

3. She fell in some _____.
   plants (mud) water flowers

Fill in the blanks.

4. She wore the mud __**hat**__ for __**three**__ years.

Make a box over the answer.

5. What is growing from the hat now?
   trees plants bugs

Fill in the blanks.

1. Who told Jean what to say if she wanted to have fun? the __**talking**__ animal

2. He said, "If you want to have fun, say '__**side slide**__.'"

3. Jean was up to her __**nose**__ in snow.

4. What do you say if you want to be cold? __**side slide**__

5. What do you say if you want to be warm again? **I want to be warm again.**

Circle the answers.

6. Did the talking animal tell the right rule about dusty paths?
   Yes (No)

7. Did he tell the right rule about having fun?
   Yes (No)

8. Make up a rule about talking animals. Talking animals _____.
   do good things (lie) tell bedtime stories

Find out where the mice are.

Rule: Every big house has mice in it.

   The boss has a little house.
   Sid has a big house.
   Ann has a big horse.
   Jean has a big house.
   Sam's house is very big.

Who has a house with mice? __**Sid**__ __**Jean**__ __**Sam**__

All dogs sleep.   Mike is a dog.

What do you know about Mike? __**He sleeps.**__

   Some animals are very small. And other animals are very big. A mouse is small. A bug is even smaller. There are animals smaller than a bug. The biggest animal that lives on land is the elephant. Every day he eats a pile of grass bigger than you are. But the elephant is not the biggest animal there is. The biggest animal is the whale. Whales do not live on land. Whales live in the sea. Some whales are bigger than ten elephants.

Fill in the blanks.

1. Is a mouse a big animal? **no**

2. Name an animal that is smaller than a mouse. **a bug**

3. Is a bug the smallest animal there is? **no**

4. What is the biggest animal that lives on land? **an elephant**

5. Name an animal that is bigger than an elephant. **a whale**

6. Where do whales live? **in the sea**

7. Some __**whales**__ are bigger than __**ten**__ elephants.

Fill in the blanks.

1. What is the rule about how to be cold? **say, side slide**

2. What do you say if you want to be warm again?
I want to be warm again.

3. What is the rule about talking animals? Talking animals **lie** .

4. If a talking animal tells you that pink ice cream is good, you know that pink ice cream is **bad** .

Make a line over the answers.

5. Who did Jean meet? a talking _____
   <u>bug</u>   tree   lady

6. The bug said, "I never _____."
   eat   <u>talk</u>   sleep

Find out who has ice cream.

> Rule: The animals that are taking a bath have ice cream.

The tiger is taking a bath.
The lion is walking with the mouse.
The cat is taking a bath.
The turtle is taking a bath.
The frog is sleeping on a log.

Who has ice cream?
the tiger   the cat   the turtle

All ticks have eight legs.   I have a tick.

What do you know about my tick? **It has eight legs.**

Trees do not grow in the winter because the ground is cold. In the spring the sun begins to make the ground warmer and warmer. First the top of the ground gets warm. Then the deeper parts of the ground get warm. Every year small trees begin to grow before big trees grow. Small trees grow first because their roots are not very deep in the ground. So their roots warm up before the roots of big trees warm up.

Fill in the blanks.

1. When do trees begin to grow? in the **spring**

2. Trees do not grow in the **winter** .

3. Trees begin to grow when their roots get **warm** .

4. Why do small trees grow first every year? **Their roots are not very deep in the ground.**

79

Fill in the blanks.

1. What is the title of this story? **She Tricks a Talking Animal**

2. What do you say if you want to be cold? **side slide**

3. What is the rule about talking animals?
Talking animals lie.

4. What do you say if you want to be warm again?
I want to be warm again.

5. Jean told the bug to tell her about something that is really **bad** .

Circle the answers.

6. What happened when Jean tapped her foot three times?
She began to _____.
sneak   snake   (fly)   cry

7. What did the strange man say to Jean?
"Arf."   "Barn, barn."   ("Bark, bark.")
"Hello, there."

Find out who is smart.

> Rule: The people with hats are smart.

Kim has a hat.
Sid has a hat.
The boss does not have a hat.
Ellen has a hat.
Spot does not have a hat.

Who is smart? **Kim   Sid   Ellen**

All bikes have wheels.   Tom has a bike.

What do you know about Tom's bike? **It has wheels.**

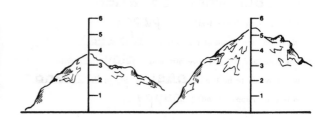

Some mountains are miles tall. The tallest mountain in the U.S. is in Alaska. It is nearly four miles tall. But it is not the tallest mountain in the world. The tallest mountain in the world is named Everest. Everest is in a land called Tibet. Everest is over five miles tall.

Fill in the blanks.

1. The tallest mountain in the U.S. is in **Alaska** .

2. How many miles tall is that mountain? **nearly four**

3. The tallest mountain in the world is in a land called **Tibet** .

4. That mountain is named **Everest** .

5. Everest is over **five** miles tall.

Circle the answers.

1. Who did Jean trick? A talking _____

   cat   rat   (bug)   bat

2. What did Jean do so that she could fly?

   said, "side, slide"   (tapped her foot three times)

Fill in the blanks.

3. What is the rule about talking animals?

   __Talking animals lie.__

4. What did the man hand Jean? __a note__

5. If you tell the man to
   become a dog, the man becomes __the word dog__.

6. Every time Jean says, "But what and when . . . ," the wizard

   __disappears__ .

7. How many more rules did Jean need
   to leave the land of peevish pets? __one__ (or **1**)

Find out who has a bug.

Rule: Every fat bottle has a bug in it.

   Pat's bottle is fat.
   Fred's bottle is not fat.
   Don's bottle is fat.
   Ellen's bottle is not fat.
   Sandy's bottle is not fat.

Who has a bug? __Pat   Don__

All dops are made of wood.   I have a dop.

What do you know about my dop? __It is made of wood.__

Do you remember which land animal is the
biggest? The elephant. Which is the biggest animal
of all? The whale. Where does the whale live? In
the sea. But a whale is not a fish. Here is the
rule: Fish breathe water. Can you breathe water?
No. Can a dog breathe water? No. Can a whale
breathe water? No. Whales must breathe air, just
like you and me. Whales have a hole at the top
of their heads. They stick their heads out of the
water and breathe air. Remember, a whale is not
a fish.

Fill in the blanks.

1. Which land animal is the biggest? __the elephant__

2. Which animal is the biggest of all? __the whale__

3. Where does the whale live? __in the sea__

4. Can you breathe water? __no__

5. Can a whale breathe water? __no__

6. A whale is __not__ a __fish__ .

80

Fill in the blanks.

1. How do you make the wizard appear?

   Say, "__I need help__ ."

2. How do you make the wizard disappear?

   Say, "__But what and when__ ."

3. What was on Jean's bed? __a puppy__

4. What was the name of the puppy? __Wizard__

5. The note said, "If you love him and __play__ with him, he

   will grow up to be the __best__ dog in the __land__ ."

6. Was Jean happy or sad? __happy__

Find out who is a boss.

Rule: Every boss has short hair.

   Tom has short hair.
   Carol has short hair.
   Ron has long hair.
   Ellen has no hair.
   Pam has short hair.

Who is a boss? __Tom   Carol   Pam__

All mups have red ears.   Ellen is a mup.

What do you know about Ellen? __She has red ears.__

The first people lived thousands and thousands
of years back. These people needed food, but they
couldn't go to the store and buy food. There were
no food stores. There were no stores of any kind.
So these people had to hunt animals. But they did
not have guns. They did not have arrows. So they
had to use rocks and sticks to kill animals. But
some animals were hard to kill. They were big and
mean. The men would hide behind trees and jump
out at the animal. Sometimes they would kill the
animal. Sometimes the animal would get away.
Sometimes the animal would kill them.

Fill in the blanks.

1. The first people lived __thousands__ and

   __thousands__ of years back.

2. Could these people buy food at a store? __no__

3. Did they have guns and arrows? __no__

4. What did they use to kill animals? __rocks__ and __sticks__

5. Sometimes they would kill the animal. But sometimes the __animal__
   would kill them.